OPERATION *CRUSADER*

DIE WEHRMACHT IM KAMPF

OPERATION *CRUSADER*: TANK WARFARE IN THE DESERT, TOBRUK 1941

HERMANN BÜSCHLEB

TRANSLATED BY DAVID DORONDO
SERIES EDITOR: MATTHIAS STROHN

CASEMATE
Philadelphia & Oxford

AN AUSA BOOK

Association of the United States Army
2425 Wilson Boulevard, Arlington, Virginia, 22201, USA

Published in the United States of America and Great Britain in 2019 by
CASEMATE PUBLISHERS
1950 Lawrence Road, Havertown, PA 19083, USA
and
The Old Music Hall, 106–108 Cowley Road, Oxford OX4 1JE, UK

Originally published as Die Wehrmacht im Kampf: Hermann Büschleb, *Feldherrn und Panzer im Wüstenkrieg: Die Herbstschlacht 'Crusader' im Vorfeld von Tobruk, 1941* (Neckargmünd: Kurt Vowinckel Verlag, 1966)

Translator: David Dorondo
Series Editor: Matthias Strohn

Hardcover Edition: ISBN 978-1-61200-723-6
Digital Edition: ISBN 978-1-61200-724-3

A CIP record for this book is available from the British Library

Printed and bound in the United States of America

Typeset in India for Casemate Publishing Services. www.casematepublishingservices.com

For a complete list of Casemate titles, please contact:

CASEMATE PUBLISHERS (US)
Telephone (610) 853-9131
Fax (610) 853-9146
Email: casemate@casematepublishers.com
www.casematepublishers.com

CASEMATE PUBLISHERS (UK)
Telephone (01865) 241249
Email: casemate-uk@casematepublishers.co.uk
www.casematepublishers.co.uk

Cover image: Bundesarchiv Bild 101I-782-0016-32A

Contents

Foreword

The War in North Africa had, to use a Clausewitzian term, its own grammar. The Axis and Allied troops that faced each other in this theatre of war did not only have to fight against the physical enemy, but also against a difficult climate. This was one of the contributing reasons why North Africa has been associated with chivalry and the honourable conduct of war. It was perceived as a war of gentlemen and thus it stood in stark contrast to the war that was waged at the same time on the Eastern Front, where two opposed extreme ideologies allowed far less room for such chivalry. The campaign in North Africa was focused for a long period on the city of Tobruk. The Germans besieged the city from April to November 1941, had to withdraw and then seized it in a swift campaign in June 1942. Operation *Crusader*, launched by the British on 18 November 1941, was part of this struggle. It broke the Axis siege of Tobruk and relieved the beleaguered city. This operation is the topic of the book that you, the reader, hold in your hands now.

However, the book is more than just an account of the operation. The author, Hermann Büschleb (1915–98) had fought in World War II and joined the new West German military, the Bundeswehr. His qualities as an officer were obvious; he ended his career as a general in the Bundeswehr, having commanded, amongst other formations, the 7th Panzergrenadier Division. Büschleb wrote his book in 1965. At that time, the Bundeswehr was fully integrated into NATO and German soldiers served alongside their now allied and former enemy counterparts from Britain. In accordance with his military training and his socialisation in the military as a highly successful staff officer, Büschleb's account of '*Crusader*' is that of a detached observer. He does not have many words for the human suffering that occurred during the battle. However, it is striking how often Büschleb speaks of heroism and of the brave conduct of the troops — on both sides. Thus, this book can also be seen as a contribution to reconciliation between the two armies. Last, but not least, there was a clear military aim that Büschleb pursued with his book. This is not merely the historical account of a staff officer. In the 1960s, the Cold War was in its heyday and German military expertise was much sought after by the Western Allies. German tactical and operational prowess shown in World War II was seen as a possible answer to the numerical superiority in men and material of the Warsaw Pact should the Cold War turn hot. This book should, therefore, also be read as an instruction manual to military personnel. Already in the introduction Büschleb hints at this. He tells the reader that history provides lessons for the present and the future. In particular, he dwells on the importance of command and leadership. The German perception, forged in two world wars, was that their command and leadership principles were superior to those of their (former) enemies. The book can thus be seen as a case study of, and almost as a textbook for, leadership and command of armoured and mechanised warfare — that type of warfare that the Bundeswehr and NATO were expecting they would have to fight against the Warsaw Pact. This intention is expressed even more clearly in his conclusion; Büschleb first describes the outcome of the battle before drawing lessons that were as applicable in the 1960s as they had been during World War II.

The book, therefore, offers far more than 'just' an analysis of Operation *Crusader*. It opens a window to military thinking of the 1960s and it shows that history really does provide lessons for the present and the future.

Dr Matthias Strohn, MSt, FRHistS
Head of Historical Analysis,
Centre for Historical Analysis and Conflict Research
Reader in Modern War Studies, University of Buckingham

Maps

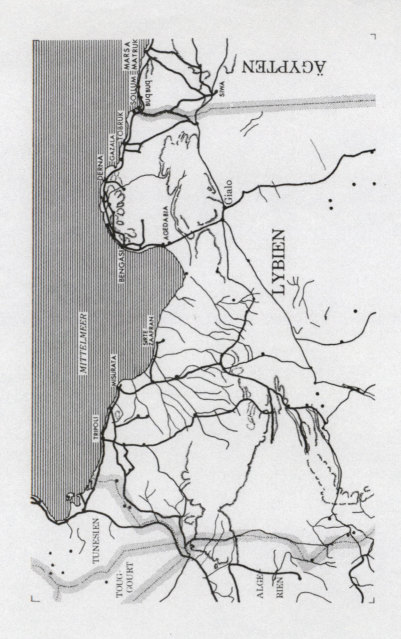

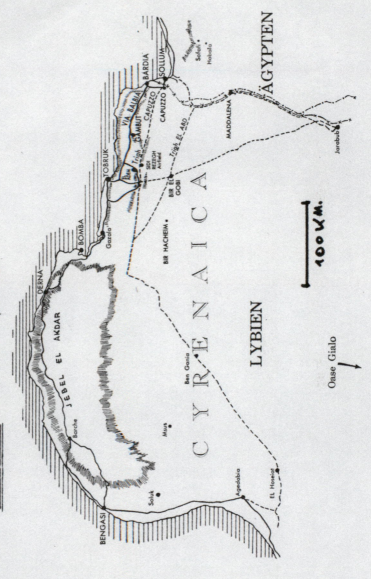

CYRENAICA – Winter 1941/1942 –

Nr. 1

BENGASI

Soluk

Barche

JEBEL EL AKDAR

DERNA

Msus

Agedabia

El Haseiat

Ben Gania

CYRENAICA

LYBIEN

Oase Gialo

100 KM.

BOMBA

Gazala

TOBRUK

Trigh

SIDI
REZEGH
Airfield

BIR HACHEIM

BIR EL
GOBI

VIA BALBIA

Trigh GAMBUT

CAPUZZO

CAPUZZO

Trigh EL ABD

BARDIA

SOLLUM

MADDALENA

Safafi

Habata

ÄGYPTEN

Jarabub

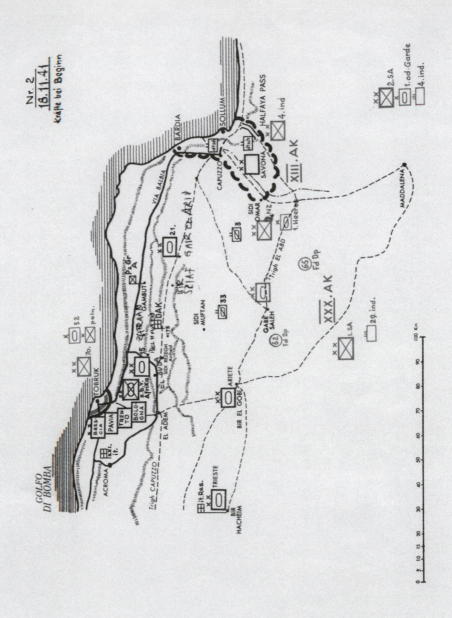

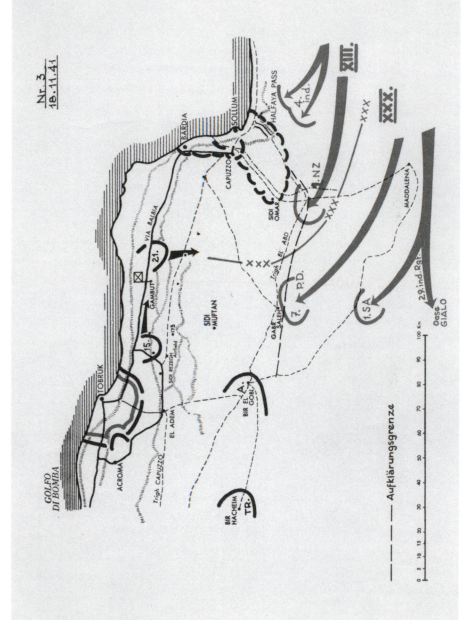

Nr. 3
18.11.41

GOLFO DI BOMBA

TOBRUK
ACROMA
EL ADEM
Trigh CAPUZZO
BIR HACHEIM
TR.
BIR EL GOBI
A.
SIDI MUFTAN
GAB.SALEH
GAMBUT
VIA BALBIA
SIDI REZEGH Airfield
•175
21.
15.
BARDIA
SOLLUM
CAPUZZO
SIDI OMAR
HALFAYA PASS
4.ind.
1.NZ
Trigh EL ABD
7. P.D.
xxx
xxx
xxx
1.SA
MADDALENA
2.9.ind.Rgt.
Oase GIALO
XIII.
XXX.

Aufklärungsgrenze

0 5 10 15 20   30   40   50   60   70   80   90   100 Km

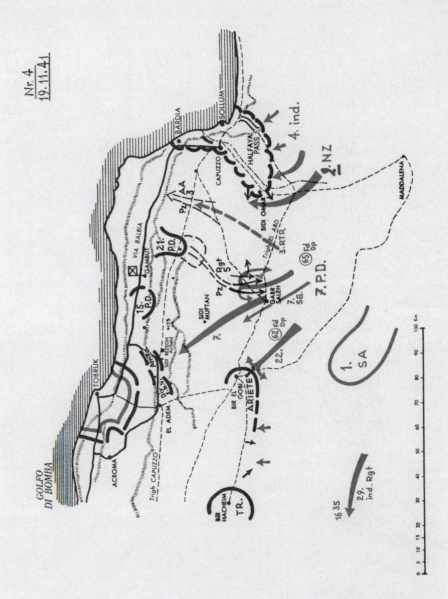

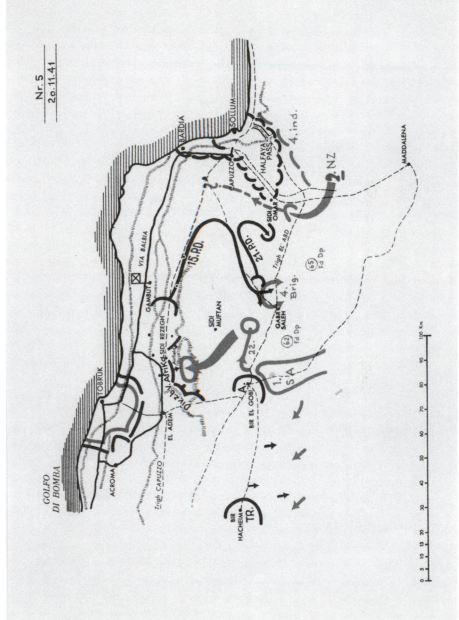

Nr. 5
2o.11.41

GOLFO DI BOMBA

TOBRUK
ACROMA
VIA BALBIA
GAMBUT
EL ADEM
SIDI REZEGH
N. AFRIKA
DIV. z. b.V.
15. P.D.
SIDI MUFTAN
22.
1. S'A
BIR EL GOBI
BIR HACHEIM
TR.
Trigh CAPUZZO
BARDIA
CAPUZZO
SOLLUM
HALFAYA PASS
4. ind.
SIDI OMAR
21. P.D.
Trigh EL ABD
4. Brig.
GARET SALEH
62 Fd Dp
65 Fd Dp
2. NZ
MADDALENA

0 5 10 20 30 40 50 60 70 80 90 100 Km

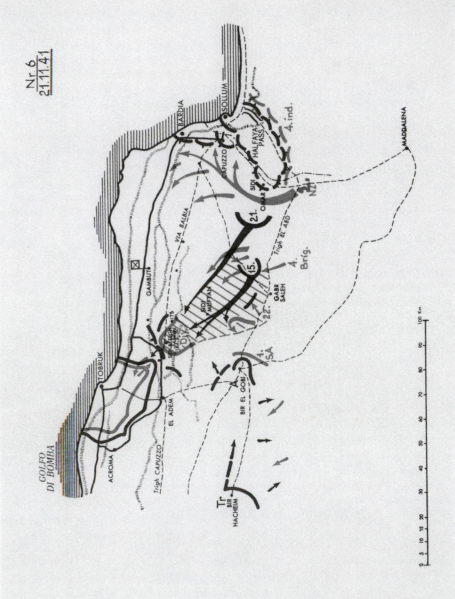

Nr. 6
21.11.41

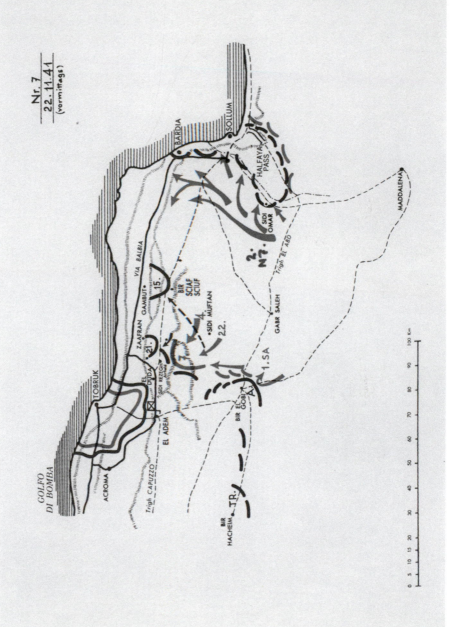

Nr. 7
22.11.41
(vormittags)

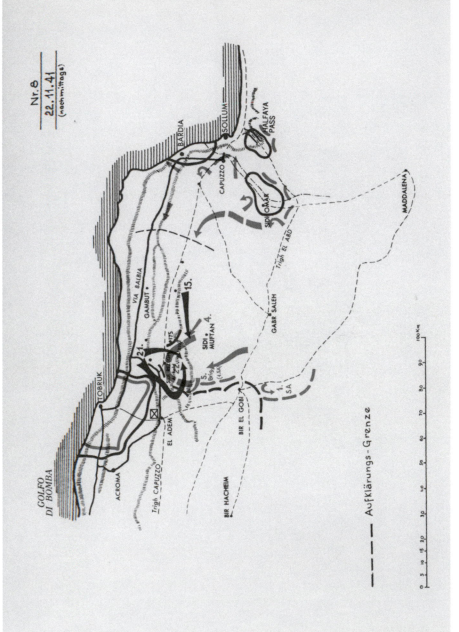

Nr. 8
22.11.41
(nachmittags)

GOLFO DI BOMBA

ACROMA

TOBRUK

VIA BALBIA

GAMBUT

Trigh CAPUZZO

EL ADEM

BIR HACHEIM

BIR EL GOBI

SIDI MUFTAN

GABR SALEH

BARDIA

CAPUZZO

SOLLUM

HALFAYA PASS

SIDI OMAR

Trigh EL ABD

MADDALENA

21.

15.

4.

5. Brig. (I.SA)

1. SA

0 5 10 15 20   30   40   50   60   70   80   90   100 Km

— — — Aufklärungs-Grenze

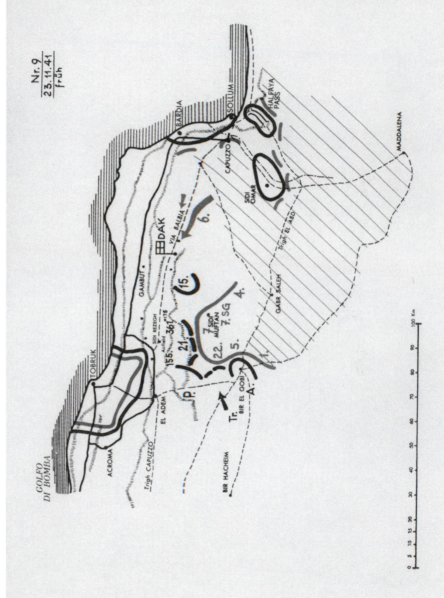

Nr. 9
23.11.41
früh

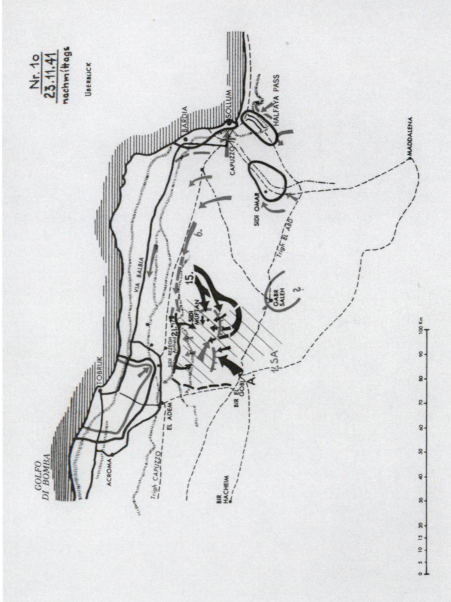

Nr. 1o
23.11.41
nachmittags

Überblick

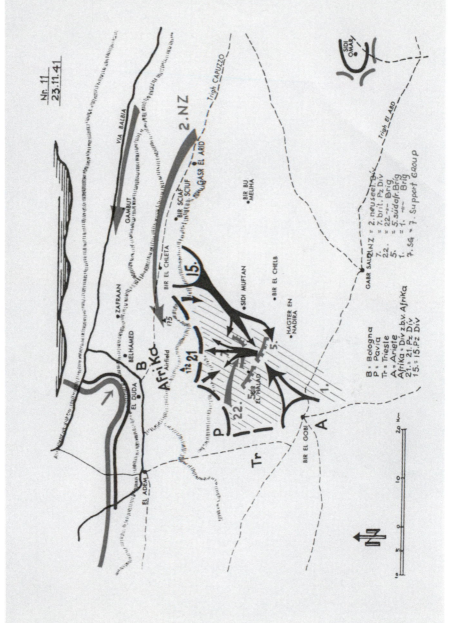

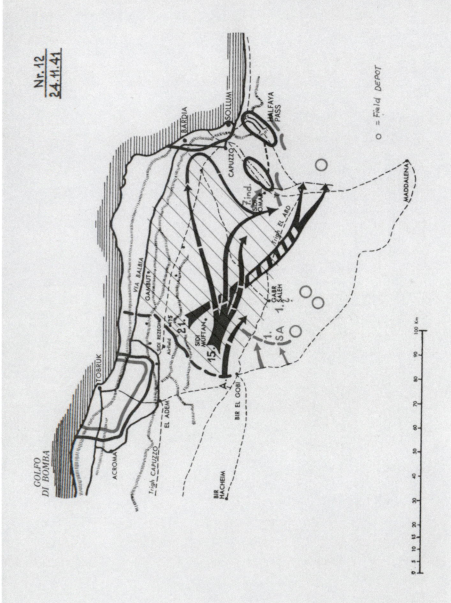

Nr. 12
24.11.41

GOLFO DI BOMBA

ACROMA

TOBRUK

EL ADEM

Trigh CAPUZZO

BIR HACHEIM

BIR EL GOBI

SIDI REZEGH

GAMBUT

VIA BALBIA

Airfield

SIDI MUFTAH

21.

15.

A.

1. SA

1. GABR SALEH

1. ?

Trigh EL ABD

SIDI OMAR

7. ind.

CAPUZZO

BARDIA

SOLLUM

HALFAYA PASS

MADDALENA

O = Field DEPOT

0 5 10 20 30 40 50 60 70 80 90 100 Km

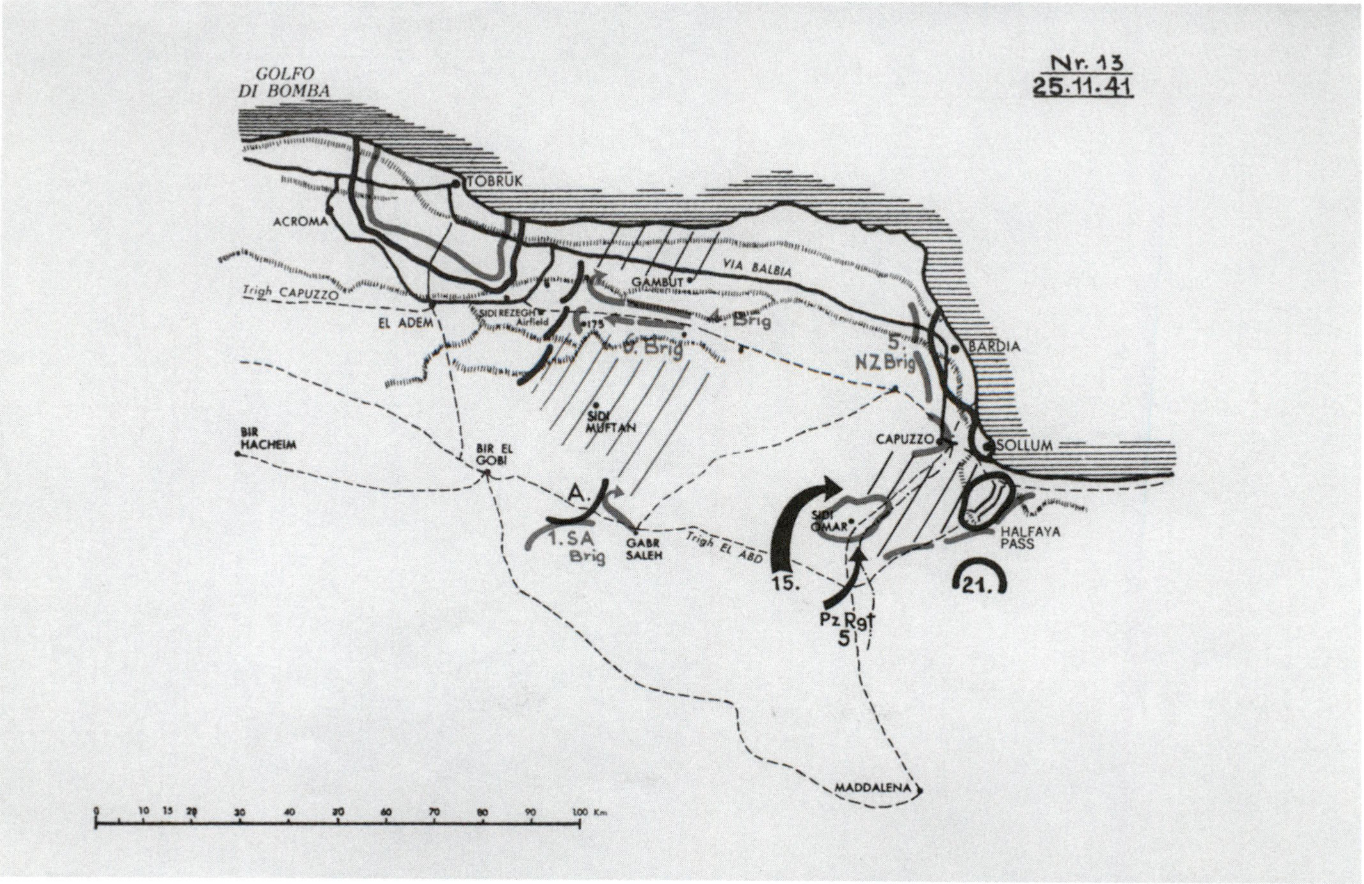

Nr. 13
25.11.41

GOLFO
DI BOMBA

TOBRUK

ACROMA

Trigh CAPUZZO

EL ADEM

SIDI REZEGH
Airfield

VIA BALBIA

GAMBUT

173

4. Brig

6. Brig

SIDI MUFTAH

BIR EL
GOBI

BIR
HACHEIM

1. SA
Brig

GABR
SALEH

A.

Trigh EL ABD

15.

SIDI
OMAR

Pz Rgt
5

CAPUZZO

5. NZ Brig

BARDIA

SOLLUM

HALFAYA
PASS

21.

MADDALENA

0   10 15 20   30   40   50   60   70   80   90   100 Km

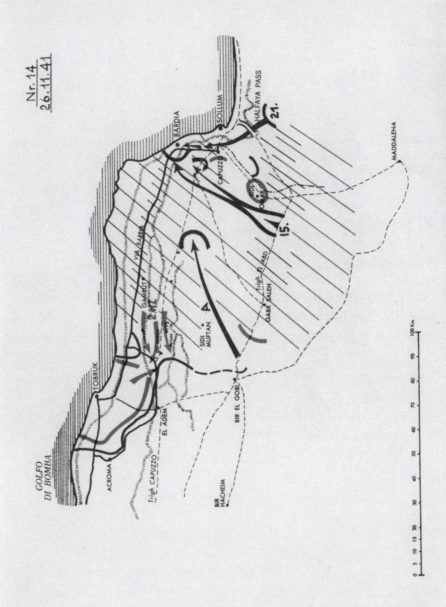

Nr. 14
26.11.41

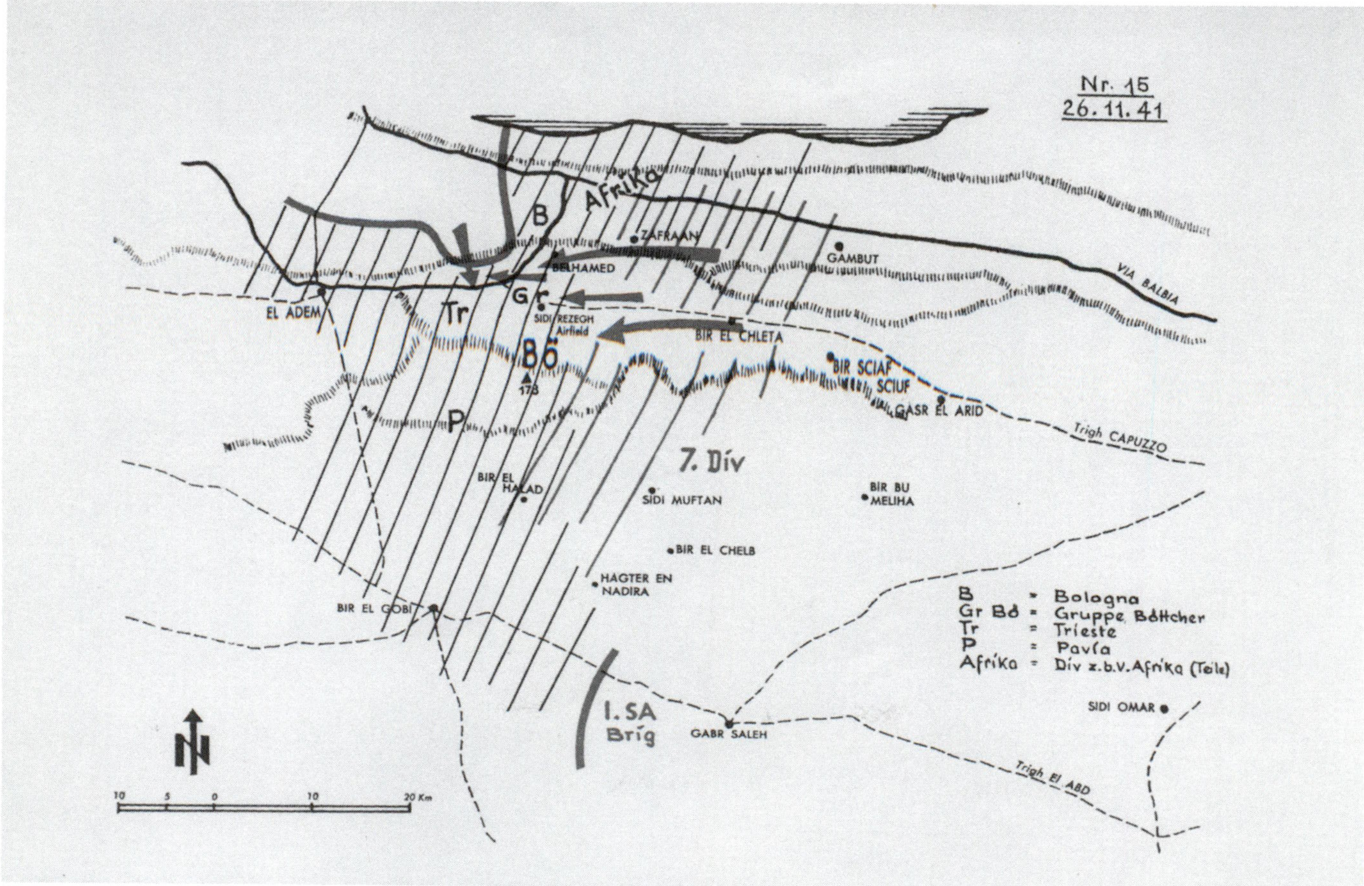

Nr. 15
26. 11. 41

VIA BALBIA

Trigh CAPUZZO

GAMBUT

BIR SCIAF SCIUF

GASR EL ARID

BIR BU MELIHA

BIR EL CHELB

7. Div

ZAFRAAN

BELHAMED

SIDI REZEGH
Airfield

SIDI MUFTAN

HAGTER EN NADIRA

BIR EL HAAD

Afrika

B

Gr

Tr

Bö

EL ADEM

BIR EL GOBI

GABR SALEH

I. SA Brig

SIDI OMAR

Trigh EL ABD

B   = Bologna
Gr Bö = Gruppe Böttcher
Tr   = Trieste
P   = Pavia
Afrika = Div z.b.V.Afrika (Teile)

N

10   5   0   10   20 Km

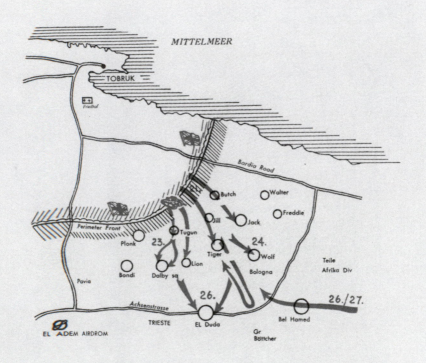

MITTELMEER

TOBRUK

Friedhof

Bardia Road

Butch   Walter

Jill   Jack   Freddie

Perimeter Front

Plonk   Tugun   23.

Tiger   24.   Wolf

Teile
Afrika Div

Pavia   Bondi   Dalby sq   Lion   Bologna

Achsenstrasse   26.   26./27.

TRIESTE   EL Duda   Bel Hamed

EL ADEM AIRDROM

Gr
Böttcher

0   2   4   6   8 Km

SIDI REZEGH AIRDROME

Nr. 17
27.11.41

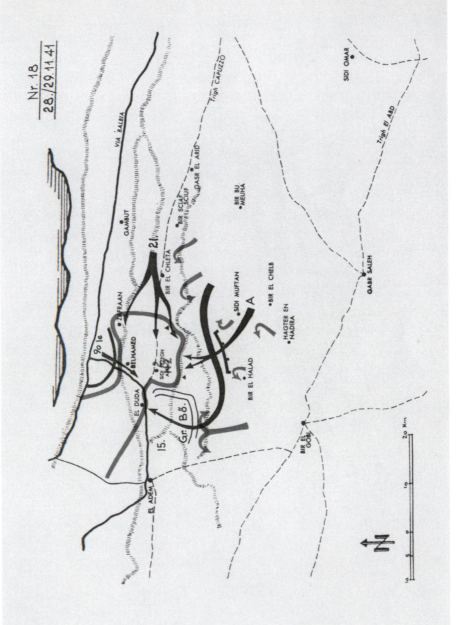

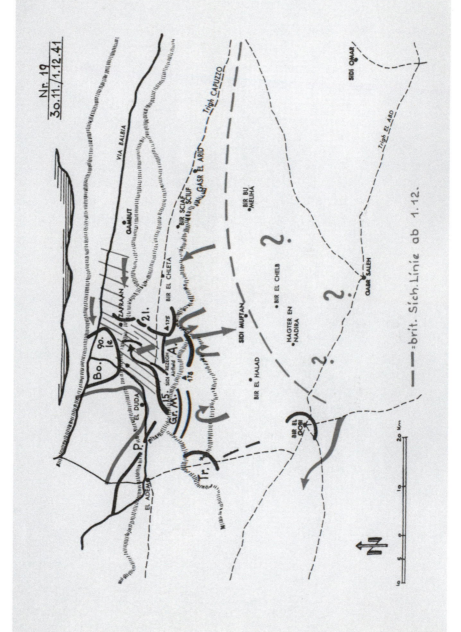

Nr. 19
30.11./1.12.41

VIA BALBIA

GAMBUT

BIR EL CHLETA

BIR SCIAF
SCIAF

Trigh CAPUZZO

GASR EL ABID

BIR BU
MELIHA

SIDI MUFTAH

BIR EL CHELB

HAGTER EN
NADIRA

SIDI OMAR

Trigh EL ABD

GASR SALEH

BIR EL HALAD

BIR EL
GOBI

EL ADEM

P. EL DUDA

Bo. 90.
le.

ZAFRAAN

21.

▲175

SIDI REZEGH
Airfield

A.

▲178

Gr. M.

Tr.

brit. Sich. Linie ab 1.12.

N

20 Km

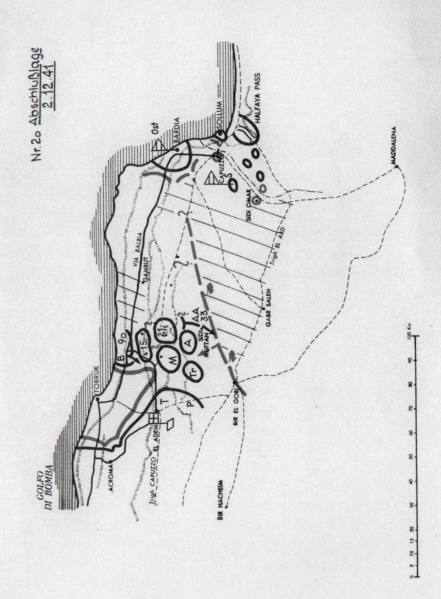

Nr. 20 Abschlußlage
2.12.41

Background

The intervention of German troops under General Rommel in 1941 threw the North African war between Britain and Italy back nearly to its starting point. The front lines ran hard by the old border between Egypt and Libya in the coastal strip between the sea and the deep desert. In Libya, the British held only Tobruk, and the city was besieged by German and Italian forces. In this situation, both sides were forced into a pause in the fighting during the summer and autumn of 1941; the British due to losses suffered in the retreat, the Axis armies due to acute logistical difficulties and the requirements of their siege of Tobruk.

For both sides, the goal remained the possession of North Africa. The Axis powers (Germany and Italy) thereby hoped to secure the Italian colonies and, especially, to block the Allied threat to Europe emanating from the whole of the Mediterranean Basin. For their part, the Allies hoped to use the occupation of North Africa to close the blockade ring from the south around the Axis powers; to protect their bases in Egypt and the Suez Canal, on Malta and at Gibraltar; and to create a strategic assembly area for future operations.

As commander of *Panzergruppe Afrika* (until then the *Deutsches Afrika-Korps*), General Erwin Rommel had largely separated himself during his operations, at least inwardly speaking, from his nominal Italian superiors. Consequently, *his* decisions were the decisive ones during the North African theatre's battles insofar as Axis forces were concerned. His initiative also influenced the directives coming from Berlin for the German troops in North Africa. In this situation, he had first to maintain the defensive effectiveness of the front at the Sollum–Halfaya Pass, near Capuzzo and near Bardia. Only when assured of the protection to the east provided by these positions could he attempt to conquer Tobruk, but the fortress had to be taken. The Germans and Italians had to possess Tobruk as a forward supply base and port before a further offensive against Egypt would be possible, an offensive whose success might be decisive for an Axis victory in North Africa. In the face of logistical difficulties, the enormous length of the Axis supply lines reaching back to Benghazi, the continuing British naval campaign being waged from Malta and Alexandria, and British air superiority, *Panzergruppe Afrika* initiated planning for the conquest of Tobruk in November 1941. In this effort, Rommel had largely striven in vain to engage the support of Italian commanders who were both his superiors and his neighbours-in-theatre. Doubts on all sides were driven by the realisation that both the Germans and Italians possessed insufficient strength of numbers and equipment. Meanwhile, the British Eighth Army in Egypt had received troops and equipment in such strength that it could plan for an offensive in mid-November that would destroy the German armoured forces, relieve Tobruk and create the conditions for a decisive victory throughout North Africa.

While the Eighth Army steadily grew in strength in the autumn of 1941 and even built a railway from Mersa Matruh (or Marsa Matruh) to the front so as to improve its logistics, the combat capability of the Axis forces could only be dearly purchased. The conquest of Malta, an island commanding the sea lanes to North Africa, had been demanded by the German side. Though seizing the island might well be of decisive influence in the desert war's outcome, that effort had been put off by the demands of the campaign in Russia that had been launched in June 1941. The disruption of Italo–German logistics became even worse with the sinking of transport ships in their repeated attempts to reach North Africa from Italy, as well as by a 50 per cent reduction in the capacity of the port of Tripoli in the wake of its harbour's bombardment by three of the Royal Navy's battleships. In September, the British sank 63,000 gross registered tons (GRT) of shipping in the sea lanes between Italy and the ports of Tripoli and Benghazi. Consequently, only about a third of German reinforcements and perhaps 15 per cent of supplies were successfully transported. About 20 per cent of all fuel shipments were also lost in September. In October, only 18,000 tons of supplies arrived safely, despite the monthly demands in Libya of between 30,000 and 40,000 tons. Only about 75 per cent of required fuel made it through. Worse, in early November, an entire convoy escorted by Italian warships was destroyed, and total losses for the month reached at least 13 ships totalling more than 60,000 GRT. These losses constituted more than 35 per cent of the entire tonnage-capacity and 62 per cent of the fuel intended for German–Italian troops in the theatre. As early as September, the German naval staff had repeatedly demanded a fundamental improvement in this situation and its urgent redressing 'if the entire North African position is not to be lost, not to mention our own offensive operations. Loss of the North African position means the loss of the whole of the Mediterranean.' Entire units and parts of units never reached North Africa. Materiel reinforcements did not get through. Fuel and ammunition had to be preserved very carefully if any offensive reserves were to be built up. Improvisation became the norm for organisation, materiel and personnel. The Axis forces' logistical situation in North Africa was already strained (when it wasn't actually breaking down altogether) by the distance of some 350km that stretched between the more-or-less functioning port of Benghazi and the area around Tobruk. Making matters even worse, significant elements of *Panzergruppe Afrika* lay up to 150km further eastward towards the border with Egypt.

Lastly, due to the earlier Balkan operations, the landings on Crete and the start of the Russian campaign (Operation *Barbarossa*), the *Luftwaffe* security that had been demanded by the Supreme Command of the Armed Forces (*Oberkommando der Wehrmacht* – OKW) could never be effectively executed. It was rumoured that Hermann Göring, commander in chief of the *Luftwaffe*, openly sabotaged the necessary orders. The principal *Luftwaffe* element available in North Africa, *Fliegerkorps X*, did not possess sufficient forces for either offensive or defensive missions over the Mediterranean, and the relative weakness of Italian naval and air forces made restoring the situation nearly hopeless. Consequently, the planned German attack on Tobruk in September had to be repeatedly postponed. Even in November, Axis combat capability and materiel reserves remained below what was necessary for a decisive success.

The Situation to 18 November 1941

In the late summer and autumn of 1941, the British government had established the Eighth Army in north-western Egypt and brought it up to a strength of four motorised divisions, one armoured division, two armoured brigades and several regiments. In addition, Eighth Army's commander, Sir Alan Cunningham, strengthened his own offensive plans behind a veil of secrecy. In the process, he collected 30,000 tons of supplies in depots – enough for a week's fighting – primarily on his southern flank, had a pipeline laid to increase the supply of fuel and established a forward railhead 120km west of Mersa Matruh. Divided into two corps, his forces stood ready to attempt to defeat Axis armies in Cyrenaica and then advance to take Tripoli. In the process, the siege of Tobruk would be lifted and the troops encircled there – the 70th Infantry Division, the 32nd Armoured Brigade and a Polish infantry brigade – would be relieved. The German supply base at Benghazi would also be eliminated. The offensive's point of main effoprt would be an attack in the direction of Tobruk, whereby enemy armoured formations would be destroyed by the British XXX Corps acting in conjunction with British units in the beleaguered city. Neighbouring XIII Corps had the task of fixing German–Italian forces on the border and breaking up both their communications and formations. As a further subsidiary attack in the south, an assault of a motorised regiment to seize the Gialo Oasis far in the Axis armies' rear was intended to cut off their possible lines of retreat to the west.

With strong support from the RAF, the beginning of the attack was planned for the morning of 18 November 1941, the approach march to the Libyan–Egyptian border having begun on 12 November. Due to well-conducted British deception plans – night marches, effective use of cover and camouflage by day, radio silence – as well as storms and rainy weather grounding Axis reconnaissance flights, German forces did not discover the British activity. Although German commanders recognised the potential threat of a British attack, the blow on 18 November nevertheless came as a surprise to Axis formations.

General Rommel, as commander of *Panzergruppe Afrika*, had reached the Libyan–Egyptian border in late summer and early autumn with the initial goal of capturing Tobruk, but since German forces in North Africa were too weak to do so alone, the support of Italian formations was required. Italian commanders, however, would only agree to the plan if corresponding reinforcements in divisions, weapons and ammunition arrived first. It was only thanks to Rommel's untiring insistence that the supreme commander of the Libyan high command, General Bastico, and the commanders of the XXI Corps in front of Tobruk and the Italian reserve corps approved the attack, even though the supplies they'd demanded had been decimated by the British fleet in the Mediterranean. The oft-postponed date for the assault on Tobruk was now set for either 21 or 23 November. Of course, those dates carried the risk that the expected attack of Eighth Army could hit the Axis forces either in their assembly areas or in their flanks once they'd opened their own action. Consequently, 21st Panzer Division was not to take part in the attack on Tobruk. By the end of October, German aerial reconnaissance had been able to gain hardly any insight into the situation in Egypt, and in any case that reconnaissance was limited by poor weather as well as by enemy air defences.

On 16 November, day-long storms and nightly rains broke over North Africa. Bridges were washed away, airfields were swamped, takeoffs and landings became impossible. It was evident that the vital aerial reconnaissance would be out of the question for the Axis for several days. On 17 November, rain fell uninterruptedly. Furthermore, the Germans observed that there was complete radio silence on the British side. In the first half of the following day, 18 November, the rain continued, and it remained impossible to fly. But in the afternoon of that day, a single report came to Rommel: long columns of tanks had been spotted moving north from the area around Giarabub. However, Rommel assumed them to be British reconnaissance elements and did not alter his preparations for his impending attack on Tobruk.

On the British side, too, the weather had affected operations. Aerial bombing raids against Axis supply lines, artillery positions, staff areas and fortified positions could not be launched on 18 November. Meanwhile, British spearheads advancing into the heights between Sidi Omar and Gabr Saleh remained unobserved. The German 33rd Armoured Reconnaissance Battalion,[1] operating west of the 3rd Armoured Reconnaissance Battalion and moving in the Trigh el Abd, merely reported contact with British reconnaissance elements in the vicinity of Gabr Saleh.

---

1   A reconnaissance detachment, an *Aufklärungsabteilung*, could notionally be as large as a battalion, and may be regarded as such.

The Situation in Context

1. Terrain

The operational area, constituting a broad strip of land between the Mediterranean coast and the interior, was up to 100km wide. To the west and to the east it is bounded by the longitude lines of Bir Hakim and Mersa Matruh, respectively. In broad stretches of this area the desert is changeable and characterised by a gravelly subsurface, sometimes mixed with sand, sometimes not. There are also small dunes and cliffs. Frequently, long stretches of this desert are covered with large stones roughly the size of human heads. Except where there is deep sand or steeply cut valleys (wadis), this terrain is generally passable for motor vehicles, but due to the lack of water, vehicular traffic typically throws up heavy dust clouds. Ground cover is essentially absent except for camel-thorn bushes and some surface grass near the coast.

Between Tobruk and Sollum, the coast is almost everywhere steep and precipitous, cut up with deep wadis and accessible only with difficulty. Particularly noteworthy are the cliffs at Sollum, separating the high plateau around Bardia and Capuzzo from the coastal plain of lower Sollum. These cliffs are traversed by the serpentine coastal highway of the Via Balbia and the road through the Halfaya Pass.[1] Numerous cliff-steps of lower elevation also run parallel to the coast. The most significant stretches from Bardia to the west and lies approximately 20–25km south of the

---

1 The Via Balbia was constructed by the Italian colonial authorities in the 1930s and named after the colonial governor-general, Italo Balbo.

coast. It is about 8km wide and ranges in height to about 60m. South of Tobruk, this feature bends to the north in the direction of the city itself. In this area, it reaches its greatest height near Sidi Rezegh and El Duda. Here there are hollows, gorges and gaps, and overhanging walls providing conditions for field camps, as well as cover from aerial observation. Movements here can be conducted without much disturbance. Towards the south, the heights are well suited to defence. Further still to the south, the desert exhibits wavelike differences in elevation and varying surfaces, as mentioned above, and remains largely traversable by vehicles.

Motor traffic preferred solid, paved roads such as the Via Balbia or the unpaved side-roads connecting the few former settlements and watering-places (for example, the track called the Trigh el Abd). The more such primitive roads were used, however, the more rutted they became. Traffic thus would become increasingly hampered in its movement. Such roads thereby became wider and wider. In the area around Tobruk, this necessitated the construction of a paved road around the besieged fortress for the purpose of resupply. That said, properly equipped motorised or mechanised troops were not always bound to the roads.

The Via Balbia remained a determining factor in the tactical consider-ations of both the Germans and British. It was the decisive supply route from the German rear. Reinforcements from Benghazi, even Tripoli, were always possible on this road. German combat forces, however, only used it when accompanied by flanking and security troops. It was not always possible to find a way to turn off the road, which raised the spectre of German forces on the road being cut off or bypassed while moving along it. By contrast, the British were more willing to send unsecured combat forces down the Via Balbia and expose their troops to the danger of being cut off that the Germans preferred to avoid. The dust clouds raised everywhere on any unpaved surface could be seen for miles. Rommel frequently used these dust clouds as a means of deception to imitate advancing motorised columns and disguise his actual movements. By the same token, they could be detected at great distance by Allied aircraft and become the target of aerial attack. Furthermore, water was always a precious commodity, despite the largely salty and sparse watering holes along the unpaved roads or the occasional wells dug by special-duty troops.

2. Weather

Winter weather in the desert of North Africa sees daily sun and temperatures up to 30°C. During the Ghibli – the seasonal south to south-westerly winds – temperatures can reach 60°C. However, nights can be distinctly cold, with temperatures falling to 5°C or even below freezing. Near the coast, winds are normally onshore during the day and offshore at night. On the whole, the climate is healthy and there is almost always dew in the morning and evening. Isolated heavy rains can occur during the winter, but are usually separated by several years at a time. These can cover wide regions, flood low-lying areas and sweep away anything in their path in gorges and gullies. In the process, they can paralyse all traffic. During the course of 17 November 1941 and the following night, heavy cloud bursts caused damaging floods and collapsed field positions. Equipment disappeared, soldiers drowned and transport columns stuck fast in the resultant mud. Tracks became bottomless slurry. Even on the following day, transport was badly hindered and aerial activity proved impossible. In the second half of November, the expected Ghibli failed to materialise, and during the fighting the weather remained warm and dry. Only on 21 November did light rain fall, and occasional cloud cover or mist (usually in the morning or afternoon) made the temperatures noticeably cooler.

3. Visibililty

In the operational area Sollum–Bir Hakim–Tobruk, sight-range extended between 4,000m and 10,000m in both the morning and afternoon. After about 1000, however, heat haze limited line-of-sight to about 3,000m. Orientation could become difficult, a condition made worse by the near vertical position of the sun, each side's poor maps, lack of visible reference points and haze–induced vagueness of contours. Darkness fell by about 1800 hours, at which point fighting usually stopped.

4. Balance of Forces

	Axis forces	Allied forces
a) Major formations	3 German divisions (12,000 men each) 5 Italian divisions (7,000)	6 divisions (14,000) 4 brigades 2 regiments
b) Formations	15 German battalions 20 Italian battalions	46 British battalions
c) Personnel Strengths		
First source group	83,000–100,000	120,000–130,000
Second source group	100,000 (approx. 50,000 Germans)	118,000
d) Armoured Strengths		
Tanks	250–280 German (nominal 360), of which ¼ Panzer IIs and 146–154 Italian	716–775
Other armoured	33 German 24 Italian	464
e) Artillery	66–90 German (nominal 93) 124 Italian	464
f) Anti-tank guns	94–136 German 195 Italian	312
g) 88mm AA gun	approx. 45 German	
h) Aircraft		
1.) Source group	120	312
2.) Source group	102 German 71 Italian	355

i) Operational movements resembled battles at sea. Most ended with the onset of darkness. The enemy rested and refitted during the hours of darkness, and occupied and supplied new assembly areas. For the individual combat soldier, runner, driver or supply technician, the enemy had to be assumed to be everywhere in the surrounding area. Established routes to neighbouring units, staff areas or strong points were not guaranteed to be free of the enemy. Engagements could occur at any time.

j) German armour officers led from the front and made independent decisions, essentially relying on broadly understood mission-command orders. British commanders remained tied to their pre-arranged battle-plans.

k) The desert imposed itself on both sides. It was every soldier's enemy. A soldier without water and a vehicle, or a tank without gasoline and ammunition, ceased to be the enemy. Consequently, the destruction of the other side's materiel was the primary intent. Attempting to conserve all resources while simultaneously attempting to exploit technical means to the greatest possible extent was essential for success by either side.

5. Weapons Comparison

a) German Panzer (Pz) II: lightly armoured, small, with the character of an armoured car on tracks, armed with a 20mm gun having no great penetrating power.

b) German Pz II	British Infantry Tank Mk II (Matilda)
Armour: 30mm	Armour: up to 50 mm in 2 ferro-concrete plates
Up to 70mm frontal and on turret	40mm side-armour (normally 40/35mm)
Gun: 50mm long-barrelled cannon	Gun: 40mm long-barrelled cannon
Could defeat all enemy armour	Could defeat enemy armour to 44mm thickness
Weight: 22.3 tons	Weight: 26–28 tons (lacked manoeuvrability)

c) German Pz IV

British Cruiser Tank Mk VI (A15 Crusader)

Armour: As on Pz III

Armour: 35mm front and turret; 25mm side

Gun: 75mm short-barrelled cannon effective against all enemy tanks except the Mark II

Opening fire (effective range 650m; total range 1,500m)

Gun: 40mm long-barrelled cannon

Faster but temperamental

Munitions: HE (tank originally conceived as artillery) and AP (though in short supply)

M3 (US)

Like the Crusader but very fast (60km/h)

Weight: 17.3 tons

Weight: 14.5 tons

d) 88mm Flak gun Opening fire (effective range 2,200m; total range 2,400m)

Far superior as anti-tank gun

3.7in anti-aircraft gun

Similar but not as mobile and positioned only around Tobruk

e) Anti-tank gun 35/36

Calibre: 37mm

Effective range: 700m

Anti-tank gun

Calibre: 2-pounder

Effective range: 700–800m (similar to the German gun)

Penetration: 51mm/90° at 500m or 43mm/60° at 500m

Munitions: HE and AP

Towed

Towed or self-propelled

Anti-tank gun 38

Calibre: 50mm

Effective range: 1,100m

Penetration: 84mm/90° at 915m or 55mm/60° at 915m

Munitions: HE and AP

Towed

f) British light artillery (8.76cm) was superior in range to the German. By contrast, the German 100mm and 150mm howitzers possessed the greater range. Superiority of German tanks was due in the first instance to better main guns (Pz III) and speed. The light anti-tank guns of the two sides were comparable.

6. British Forces

Commander Middle East: General Claude Auchinleck, headquarters in Cairo

    a) British Eighth Army (fully motorised); headquarters in Sidi Barani. Commander General [Sir] Ian Cunningham; after 27 November 1941, General Neil Ritchie

    1.) *Organisation*

        Tobruk garrison, Major General Leslie Morshead

            70th Infantry Division (14th, 16th, 23rd Infantry Brigades), Major General Ronald Scobie

            32nd Armoured Brigade, Brigadier A. C. Willison; Polish Brigade Group, Major General Stanislaw Kopanski

        Attacking forces on the right

            XIII Corps; Lieutenant General Reade Godwin-Austen (heavy infantry)

            2nd New Zealand Division (4th, 5th, 6th Brigades), Major General Bernard Freyberg

            4th Indian Division (5th, 7th, 11th Brigades), Major General Frank Messervy

            1st Army Tank Brigade, Brigadier H. R. B. Watkins

            12th Anti-aircraft Brigade

        Attacking forces on the left

            XXX Corps, Lieutenant General Willoughby Norrie (heavy armour)

7th Armoured Division, Major General William Gott

1st South African Division (1st, 5th Brigades), Major General George Brink

22nd Guards Brigade (only for security missions), Brigadier John Marriott

Reserve

2nd South African Division (3rd, 4th, 6th Inf. Brigades), Major General Isaac de Villiers

4th Indian Regiment

Oasis Group (Force E), Brigadier Denys Reid
Reinforced 29th Indian Inf. Brigade (regimental-strength)
With 6th, 7th South African Armoured Car Regiment (2 companies)
3rd Battalion, 2nd Punjab Regiment
2nd South African Field Artillery Regiment (battalion-strength)
1st Company, 73rd Anti-tank Battalion

2.) *Wartime Organisation of 7th Armoured Division*

Largest unit. Consisted of approximately 14,000 men and some 500 tanks, each brigade deploying more tanks than a German armoured division.

4th Armoured Brigade (3rd Royal Tank Regiment, 5th Royal Tank Regiment, 8th Hussars; equipped with US M3 tanks), Brigadier Alexander Gatehouse

7th Armoured Brigade (2nd Royal Tank Regiment, 6th Royal Tank Regiment, 7th Hussars), Brigadier George Davy

22nd Armoured Brigade (2nd Hussars, 3rd Yeomanry, 4th Yeomanry), Brigadier John Scott-Cockburn

Division Support Group (infantry, artillery, anti-aircraft and anti-tank guns), Brigadier 'Jock' Campbell

11th Hussars (reconnaissance)

Other elements

3.) *Armament* (Numbers in parentheses are approximate. As long as official figures for actual strengths are unavailable, after-action reports or veterans' accounts differ. Sources tend towards reporting one's own side's strength at actual levels but the enemy's at his official establishment levels. The latter are characteristically higher.)

a) Tanks

Matildas (heavily armoured infantry tank; 40mm frontal and turret armour; 35mm side armour on Mark II; slow and not manoeuvrable; Valentines, same class but with 30mm armour on average) (213/216)

Crusaders (Mark VI? [*sic*]) (fast medium tanks; 35mm frontal and turret armour; 20mm side armour) and Cruisers (Mark I) (small, fast, weakly armoured, older model) (370/335)

Stuarts (US 'Honeys') (35mm frontal armour; 20mm side armour; fast, reliable, but short-ranged) (165/165)

Light tanks (old model without combat power) (25)

Totals: 773/716 (of these totals, the numbers in Tobruk: 69/96)

b) Armoured Cars

Only in the 7th Armoured Division and the Oasis Group, including armoured prime movers and command cars (180/464)

c) Artillery

Most 18-pounders and 25-pounders (87.6mm) and employable as anti-tank guns (464/488)

d) Anti-tank guns

Most 2-pounder and 2.5-pounder (312/536)

e) Anti-aircraft guns

Most of light calibre (416)

f) Reserves

Tanks and armoured vehicles (259)

Still aboard ship (96)

In the battle's first weeks, replacements were sent
forward from these stocks, particularly to the 7th
Armoured Division.

b) *Mentality and Way of Fighting*

Extensive desert experience, composure and a near fatalism were given
substance by the optimistic expectation of victory. Notably, a schematic
approach was viewed as unavoidable in the step–by–step accomplishment
of the mission. Thus, all leaders held fast to the army's rigid plan of
attack for the first 10 days. The plan's daily objectives were retained even
in the face of situations that were completely different from what had
been anticipated. In many cases, details took precedence over the larger
picture. Direction, lines and conception blurred. Little room remained
for leaders' independent action, but it nevertheless occurred and produced
bravery. As Rommel observed: 'Their ponderous and rigid technique
of command, their over-systematic issuance of orders down to the last
detail giving little freedom of action to lower commanders; and their
limited ability to adjust to changing situations during the battle were all
equally to blame for their failure.'

c) *Airpower* (approximately 1,100 aircraft), General Cunningham

Air superiority lay on the British side. Every day, after 0500 hours,
three or four aircraft would fly multiple reconnaissance missions over the
battlefield. German movements were observed. Low-level aerial attacks
badly affected supply columns, particularly on the Via Balbia. Strafing
of individual Axis vehicles was not unheard of, and resupply vehicles
suffered significant losses. Bombers most often appeared 18 machines at
a time to attack armoured formations, depots and troops at rest.

7. German–Italian Forces

Supreme Commander Libya: General Ettore Bastico

A. Ground Forces

a) *Panzergruppe Afrika*, General Erwin Rommel
   Deutsches Afrika Korps (*DAK*), General Ludwig Crüwell

> 21st Panzer Division (5th Light Division), General Johann von Ravenstein
>
> 15th Panzer Division, General Walter Neumann–Silkow
>
> 90th Light Division (Division *zb V Afrika*), General Max Sümmermann with the bulk on the Tobruk front (e.g. 155th and 361st Infantry Regiments); elements as oases company (*Kampfgruppe Daumiller*); two battalions on the Sollum front

Corps troops including 475th Intelligence Detachment, rear-area combat-service support, and water supply elements

> Sollum front
>> *Savona* Division (Italian), General Fedele de Giorgis
>>
>> Two German battalions
>>
>> XXI Corps (Italian), General Enea Navarini
>>> *Brescia* Division (Italian), General Bortolo Zambon
>>>
>>> *Trento* Division (Italian; partially motorised), General Giuseppe de Stefanis
>>>
>>> *Pavia* Division (Italian), General Antonio Franceschini
>>>
>>> *Bologna* Division (Italian), General Alessandro Gloria

> Army-level elements
>> 104th Artillery Command, I/18 Flak Detachment, 900th Combat Engineer Battalion, I/33 Flak Detachment, 605th Anti-tank Detachment, 606th Flak Battalion, 580th Reconnaissance Company, 612th Flak Battalion, 300th Special Duty Battalion, 11th Observation Detachment, coast artillery, 10th Communications/Intelligence Regiment, 3/56 Surveillance Company, army supply units, and rear-area army command

b) *Reserve Corps* (XX Italian), General Gastone Gambarra

Ariete Armoured Division, General Mario Balotta

Trieste Armoured Division, General Alessandro Piazzoni

c) *Command Organization* (18 November 1941)

DAK (15th and 21st Panzer Divisions)

XXI Corps (Division *zbV Afrika* and the *Bologna*, *Trento*, *Brescia* and *Pavia*

Divisions)

Eastern District (*Abschnitt*)

Italian garrison at Bardia (General M. Schmidt), 104th Infantry/Rifle Regiment (from 21st Panzer Division), elements of *300. Bataillon ZbV*, a German coast artillery battery

Commandant, Army Rear Area

Liaison with Italian reserve corps and *Fliegerführer Afrika*

d) *Wartime Organization of 15th and 21st Panzer Divisions* (Appendices 2 and 3)

e) *Armament*

1. German tanks

Pz II, 20mm heavy machine gun (63/70)

Pz III, 50mm gun (some short-barrelled) (136/139)

Pz IV, 75mm gun (50/418/35)

2. Italian tanks (146)

M 13/40, obsolete, slow, limited armour, 47mm gun, weight 14tons, obstacle to effective armoured attack

Light tanks (91), no combat effectiveness, suitable only for reconnaissance

3. Artillery

German light howitzer (105mm) (48)

German heavy howitzer (150mm) (20)

German cannon (100mm) (16)

German mortars (210mm) (9)

German coast–artillery guns (69)

Italian light artillery (180/212)

Italian heavy artillery (*Panzergruppe Afrika* reported
324)
4. Anti-tank guns
37mm (33)
50mm long-barrelled (101)
75mm (2)
5. Flak guns
88mm (24/45)
6. Assessment of Numbers and Strengths

The numbers of tanks indicated here do not necessarily correspond to units' strengths as indicated in formal wartime tables of organisation and equipment (TOEs). Changeable maintenance requirements, breakdowns and occasional materiel replacements determined daily combat strengths, including on 18 November 1941. The German Pz IIIs (when they were 'up gunned') and Pz IVs – approximately 150 in all – were superior to their British counterparts. They were faster and the main guns had longer range. They could stop British tanks well beyond the latter's maximum effective range and outmanoeuvre them tactically. Only attrition shifted the tactical balance in favour of the British and their greater numbers.

f) *German Mentality and Fighting Style*

Good doctrine and training in mission-command (*Auftragstaktik*) allowed for flexibility and improvisation on the part of all leaders. Trust in their weapons gave firmness to units. Disadvantages were minimised in reconnaissance, aerial support, experience in the desert and facility with equipment. Those that remained were to be overcome through sheer physical effort. The Germans' battle morale was to be explained more by national character than in terms of sport.

As Brigadier Campbell noted: 'No one can really describe the technique of the German tank arm, as it was dominated by a singular characteristic, namely a lack of uniformity. Its methods repeated themselves only very occasionally. The [Germans'] extensive study of armour's employment, together with … combat experience gave the panzer arm a proficiency which showed itself in every battle it fought. This guaranteed a combat organization corresponding exactly with the demands of any specific situation and terrain.'

Massing at the battle's point of main effort was decisive. Since its objective was to attack the enemy in detail, the chance always existed to be superior to him at the point of contact. Combat elements moved primarily in open order. Tank units marched in a front stretching 2–4km and in a sort of checkerboard arrangement 20–30 m deep. They proceeded straight across the desert and directly at the enemy. Flanking and/or encircling movements were initiated from the operational depth. Almost all armoured units were accompanied by 88mm flak guns, often just one, in the anti-tank role. The weapon's range, its ability to open fire early and its accuracy generally forced enemy tanks onto the defensive and into acts of desperation. The absence of aerial superiority, however, hindered operational – if not always tactical – exploitation of local success. Paltry reconnaissance served as no good basis for operational decision–making. German leadership was essentially blind in this respect since the reconnaissance elements of even the large manueuvre elements were quickly exhausted in the desert's vastness.

B. Air Forces

1) *Fliegerführer Nord-Afrika* (German), General Hans Seidemann (and attached to *X Fliegerkorps*), *ca.* 106 aircraft.
     1 long-range reconnaissance squadron, Ju 88s
     1 close reconnaissance squadron
     1 fighter group (from the 53rd Fighter Wing 'Ace of Spades'), Me 109s
     2 dive-bomber groups, Ju 87s and Ju 88s
     1 destroyer (heavy fighter) group, Me 110s
     1 desert emergency squadron, Fieseler 'Stork' liaison/medevac aircraft
     135th Flak Regiment (two battalions)
     1 *Luftwaffe* Intelligence detachment
2) Italian Air Forces, *ca.* 70 aircraft
     1 reconnaissance wing
     1 fighter wing, Macchi 200s
     1 bomber group
3) Total strength: 120–200 aircraft

4) In 1941, the German *X Fliegerkorps* suffered a natural reduction in strength as it was forced to transfer units to the Eastern Front despite also being tasked with its continuing missions in the Mediterranean. These missions included: supporting the *Afrika Korps*; reinforcing Italian maritime convoy escorts; combating British naval units and maritime links in the Eastern Mediterranean; isolating Malta and preparing the reduction of the air bases on the island.

This combination of strategic, operational, and tactical missions overburdened *X Fliegerkorps*, particularly as the demands made by the campaign in Greece and then the invasion of the USSR pushed the strategic centre of gravity to the east. This shift short-changed subsequent operations in the Mediterranean.

5) The larger Mediterranean theatre consumed both German and Italian air power. Direct support of North African operations thus became dependent upon the entire theatre's demands. The decision to spread air bases all over southern Italy, Greece, Sicily and North Africa made air support highly variable in effectiveness.

6) In the North African combat zone, British air forces always enjoyed at least a five-fold superiority. German aerial reconnaissance was consequently insufficient and German attacks against ground targets occurred only infrequently. For its part, fighter activity consisted primarily of individual efforts. Appreciable support for Axis ground forces failed to materialise.

7) Air–ground cooperation existed only at the command-level of *Fliegerführer Nord-Afrika* and the *Panzergruppe*, and air liaison officers were not seconded. There was no air combat-control from the battlefield itself.

8) Despite orders from the *Oberkommando der Wehrmacht* (OKW), reinforced protection of convoys from Italy to North Africa could not be guaranteed. That could be achieved only to about Benghazi.

C. German–Italian Relations

Even though the operational theatre, climate and enemy were the same for Germans and Italians, battles demonstrated differing outcomes for the two armies. Despite long experience in North Africa, Italian forces found themselves worse equipped in all arms and equipment than their German counterparts. Making matters worse in these battles was the Italian armoured troops' lack of effective tanks and their having been largely unmechanised. Improvisation in battle demands, good training, dependable relationships between officers and other ranks, and especially the habit of self-reliance among junior leaders: these characteristics were largely unknown in Italian military training. Italian officers enjoyed significantly better rations than other ranks, even in combat, and Italian commanders demonstrated too-systematic an approach. In cases where combat required them being mixed with German troops, Italian units showed battle-worthiness. By contrast, unexpected situations and/or feelings of combat inferiority led to outbreaks of mass psychosis.

Among themselves, regular soldiers of the two armies were always comradely. Higher Italian commanders, however, were subject to a combination of awe and envy regarding their German counterparts. These Italian officers had the feeling that they were lesser in importance. On the other hand, Rommel did not trust Italian officers' insight into aggressive, mobile, armoured warfare. He would keep his plans from them for as long as he could, resulting in bitterness and impaired cooperation.

In Tobruk, where before the war the Italians had constructed extensive, concretised trenches, strong points and anti-tank ditches, the British executed an effective defense. German assaults had twice failed to carry those defences. The combination of anti-tank guns, artillery and dug-in tanks had given the Germans some unpleasant surprises. For their part, German positions lay in the area, and along the periphery, of the triangle formed by the line Bardia–Halfaya Pass–Sidi Omar. The very size of the area demanded that only strong points would be possible for defence. As a rule, these were bolstered by artillery and individual tanks, while troops manned dug-in positions. Mutual support was not always possible. Instead, scout troops maintained contact between the positions. Enemy penetration of the line and the isolation of individual positions could not be ruled out. To help in the defence, minefields of varying density were laid. In addition, the Italian *Savona* Division was deployed primarily in Sollum and Bardia.

8. Positions

a) Strategic Problems

Axis armies were supplied by way of a short but dangerous sea route from Italy to Libya, one that remained insecure. In view of the European-wide situation, control of the Mediterranean was recognised as an objective of the first rank. Nevertheless, the Axis' fixation on the war on the European continent meant that insufficient forces were available for the elimination of Malta as a British base or for the destruction of British naval and air forces on and over the Mediterranean.

By contrast, British forces relied on secure but extremely long supply lines circumnavigating Africa. It nonetheless became evident that continuous resupply not only made it possible for the British to fight in North Africa according to plan, but also allowed them to launch large-scale offensives unhindered by the sorts of factors that repeatedly forced Rommel to concede both time and numbers. That he was so compelled, in turn, forced him to become a master of improvisation. He could not do otherwise than to regard Libya specifically as a major area of operations, even though Hitler and the *OKW* viewed it as secondary in importance and ignored Italian wishes. The result was a German waging of war that did not want to take account of the supply situation. Instead, it took advantage of whatever momentary development permitted either offensive or defensive tactical action. In the long run, the Axis was more or less able to execute a strategic defensive in North Africa, one in which tactical offensives might well be justified but also one in which continuous support for larger operations over time could not be maintained.

b) German Supply

In general, German units possessed satisfactory numbers of supply personnel. However, there remained the problem of mastering the difficulty of moving supplies from the ports of Benghazi and Tripoli to the front lines. Initially, the distance was manageable, particularly in view of the Via Balbia, which provided a good route and, therefore, a beneficial influence on both transport capacity and time. Fuel, ammunition, food, water and spare parts went one way, and the wounded and sick the other.

Nevertheless, resupply to the forward units did not always keep pace with the latter's movements. Here and there, resupply with ammunition, fuel and spare parts suffered from temporary bottlenecks. These arose from Rommel's waging of mobile warfare with its high demands on these critical items, along with the decimation of the transport area.

Consequently, at the beginning of the major assault on Tobruk, prepositioning of supplies permitted an eight-fold reserve of fuel and a five- to seven-and-a-half-fold reserve of ammunition for all weapons. Forward-based dumps were established near Gambut, for example at El Adem. From there, supply columns went generally into the open desert until they located their assigned units, often as far as 100km distant. Resupply within divisions and battle groups was well integrated. In this respect, the ability of supply columns and their leaders, as well as their specialised technicians, was crucial in maintaining mobility on the battlefield for the combat units.

c) Italian Supply

In general terms, the same conditions applied to the Italians as to the Germans. Given the simpler weaponry and lack of full motorisation of Italian units, supplying them was almost always a solvable problem, provided faulty organisational planning did not occur.

d) British Supply

The British Eighth Army was brought to the greatest strength through systematic supply of weaponry and equipment. Supply problems were avoided through the construction of the Egyptian coastal road to Sofafi and the timely building of forward-based depots for fuel and ammunition in the area between Mersa Matruh, Fort Maddalena and Bir el Gubi. These depots were never discovered by Axis forces.

e) Repair and Maintenance

German repair and recovery services were used to following close on the heels of the tank companies. They achieved astounding results through improvisation. The British, for their part, used their long-distance, integrated supply services to maintain combat-effectiveness more through the bringing up of replacement vehicles than recovery and repair of damaged ones.

The Germans alone employed tank-depot repair companies using flat-bed trucks of up to 18 tons (8, 12, 18). German armoured strength was maintained only through the immediate recovery of disabled vehicles and their rapid repair while still at the front. The equipment of 15th Panzer Division's repair company was captured by the British near the coast north-west of Gambut in the first days of December 1941. Only in early 1942 were similarly equipped British tank companies themselves captured. They were found to be organised precisely on the German model.

9. Maps

Italian maps showed errors of up to 20km. By contrast, British maps were very precise and included coloured terrain features (e.g. accessibility for tanks). The grid pattern of these British maps was exact, and orientation points such as cairns were indicated by coordinates.

10. Clock Times

Times indicated herein are oriented to Western European time, one hour behind Central German time.

The Course of the Battle

A. The British Eighth Army Launches the Attack

Initially intended as the spearhead of the army, the British 7th Armoured Division was deployed widely with the objective of linking up as directly and rapidly as possible with Tobruk's besieged garrison. The division's offensive plan envisioned using 4th Armoured Brigade on the right to secure the vicinity of Gabr Saleh to the north and maintaining contact with XIII Corps' engagement. In the centre, 7th Brigade would seize Sidi Rezegh and the German airfield there. On the left, 22nd Brigade would secure the southern flank by driving on Bir el Gubi. This plan forced the division to attack on a broad front. Gaps between the brigades were to be accepted since coordination of fire and manoeuvre, as well as cooperation among the brigades, would be essentially impossible if all commanders executed their orders according to plan. At the beginning of the battle, however, this condition proved advantageous to the British; information coming into *Panzergruppe Afrika* as a result of enemy contact seemed to indicate that three so widely dispersed movements had to be simply armed reconnaissance.

In reality, the whole of the British 7th Armoured Division came on by way of Maddalena and into the area around Gabr Saleh. First contact was made about 20km east of that point on 19 November by 4th Brigade's 3rd Royal Tank Regiment (RTR). The regiment engaged the German 3rd Armoured Reconnaissance Detachment, a battalion-sized element, and drove it north-eastward to the area of Gasr el Arid. The brigade's main body reached a point north-east of, and close to, Gabr Saleh without making enemy contact. In the meantime, the British 7th Brigade had pushed forward to the area around the airfield at Sidi Rezegh, its 6th RTR in the van, also essentially without enemy contact. There, however, it surprised the close-security elements of the 361st *Afrika* Regiment. The British went into defensive positions to allow their echeloned following forces to come up. Further to the west and after midday, the British 22nd Brigade launched a bold attack – its first since the brigade's establishment – against the Italian *Ariete* armoured division's positions near Bir el Gubi. Nevertheless, the bravery of the Italian soldiers fended off the assault, with Italian troops reporting the destruction of five British tanks during their successful defence. The 22nd Brigade, however, lost a total of between 45 and 52 armoured vehicles, against which there were 45 losses on the Italian side. This first test of crews and machines was not surprising, and the bulk of the tanks on both sides would be combat–ready again in coming days.

Before midday on 19 November, the German command did not have a clear picture of the situation. Nevertheless, it ordered 21st Panzer Division to attack and destroy the reconnaissance forces presumed to be operating between Sidi Omar and Gabr Saleh and then to go over to the defence of the latter position. At the same time, 15th Panzer Division was ordered to take up positions of readiness to the south-west of Gambut.

For the attack, 21st Panzer Division had a battle group consisting of the 5th Panzer Regiment plus a detachment of 12 light field-howitzers and four flak guns of 88mm calibre. Followed by the mass of the division, this battle group met the British 4th Armoured Brigade (minus 3rd RTR) at about 1530 hours approximately 8km north-east of Gabr Saleh. Attacking straight off the march, and in heavy fighting, the German forces drove the British brigade southward over the Trigh el Abd. With minimal losses (one Pz II and two Pz IIIs), 21st Panzer reported the destruction of 23 Stuart tanks (British sources put the loss at 42) and that night took up a hedgehog position east of Gabr Saleh (35km west of Sidi Omar). The British 4th Armoured Brigade, battered as it was, withdrew to the south. Contact with the enemy was thus lost.

Meanwhile, German aerial reconnaissance had reported enemy columns deep in the desert getting under way from the Giarabub oasis and, at about 1635, from positions approximately 30km south of Bir Hakim, heading west. This was the 29th Indian Regiment on the march towards Gialo and Benghazi. *Panzergruppe Afrika* could field no forces against these formations and had to rely on strikes against them by bombers and fighter-bombers. The British XIII Corps was also on the move. The 2nd New Zealand Division struck out systematically, though haltingly, towards the north from a position west of Sidi Omar. In the process, firefights resulted with German and Italian reconnaissance elements.

The overall extent and direction of the British attack remained unclear to the Germans. By the same token, however, British commanders remained uncertain about the extent of the German defences. The surprisingly heavy Axis counter-attack against 4th Armoured Brigade nevertheless led them to expect further reactions. The fighting of 19 November witnessed a surprisingly successful advance by the British Eighth Army to within 15km of Tobruk. However, the day also saw the near complete destruction of 4th Armoured Brigade by the *Afrika Korps* deep in the area of XXX Corps. On both sides, the extent of their respective successes was underestimated due to insufficient reconnaissance and an inability to perceive clearly the enemy's operational and tactical intent. Thus, both sides also failed to develop proper tactical conceptions for the following day. During the night from 19–20 November, the weakened British 4th Armoured Brigade assembled south-east of Gabr Saleh. The 22nd Brigade broke contact with the Italian *Ariete* Division, and the 7th Support Group – along with the remaining elements of the British 7th Brigade – aimed for the airfield at Sidi Rezegh. The British expected a German counter-attack there on the morning of 20 November, mainly from either the west or the north.

In fact, General Rommel had ordered the Special Duty Division *Afrika* [Division *zbV Afrika*; later redesignated the 90th Light Division – *Trans.*] to execute an active defence. To the *Afrika Korps* as whole he could only assign the general mission that enemy forces found between Gabr Saleh and Sidi Omar be destroyed on 20 November. The *DAK*'s commanding general thereupon decided to concentrate his main formations in the direction of Sidi Omar. He was no doubt persuaded to do so by his assumption that the principal enemy forces would be found in that area. Playing a role in this decision was the evaluation – in fact an overestimation – of reports from Panzer Reconnaissance Detachment 3 and its engagement with, and subsequent avoidance of, the British 3rd RTR on 19 November. That regiment, however, had already gone to rejoin its parent brigade south-east of Gabr Saleh.

On the morning of 20 November, 21st Panzer Division began searching for enemy forces in the direction of Sidi Aziz but encountered none. Following that move, the division swung around to the south. Approximately 20km north-west of Sidi Omar, however, the division was forced to halt its desert march due to lack of fuel. Aerial resupply failed, despite its being urgently requested. Only late that night could support columns reach the stranded division. Here one sees clearly that resupply must also always accommodate itself to the demands of mobile warfare. Indeed, the supply columns which had been travelling for weeks on the Trigh Capuzzo never did find 5th Panzer Regiment on 19 November. Only the employment of radio-equipped search parties made it possible to rein in the fuel shipments before they themselves ran into enemy forces along the Trigh el Abd. Thereafter, the shipments were successfully redirected to the division on the evening of 20 November. As is so often the case, finding directions in the desert at night depended on tracking the intensity of radio signals and the use of flares and vehicles' searchlights. After a few nights' worth of enforced practice at these skills, the system of battlefield resupply almost always succeeded. That said, it remained the case that unfavourable disposition of fuel in the *Panzergruppe*'s camps, as well as the resulting long distances that fuel resupply vehicles were forced to travel, meant that this fuel still sometimes arrived late at the combat elements.

Independent of this problem, 15th Panzer Division moved out in search of the enemy from the divisional area 13km south-west of Gasr el Arid. It advanced as far as Sidi Aziz and in a large curving movement to the south-west. In the process, the division finally contacted the enemy north-east of Gabr Saleh, namely the British 4th Armoured Brigade. In a brief but heavy firefight lasting until darkness fell, the British brigade was once again driven back, this time southwards across the Trigh el Abd, and once again British forces lost a number of tanks. From an initial total strength of some 165 tanks (that morning about 123), the number fell to about 68. During the battle, the 2nd New Zealand Division had stood by only about 10km to the east with the mass of its units. However, its offer of assistance was refused by the commander of 4th Armoured Brigade on the grounds that the operational plan prohibited elements of XIII Corps being drawn into an armoured battle. Still recovering from the fighting of 19 November, the British 22nd Brigade, for its part, only began to move in the afternoon in support of the battle from the area north-east of Bir el Gubi. Ordered towards Gabr Saleh, the brigade did not arrive before darkness fell, and it only assembled fully at first light on 21 November north-west of that location.

In the defensive fighting around the airfield at Sidi Rezegh, the two regiments of the Special Duty Division *Afrika* (155th Rifle Regiment and 361st *Afrika* Regiment) were hard pressed. The regiments' anti-tank guns were relatively few, but, supported by a detachment of 88mm flak batteries and with the reinforced 3rd Armoured Reconnaissance Detachment as left-flank guard, the troops managed to prevent a breakthrough of the British combat groups to Tobruk. Admittedly, the British 7th Armoured Division strengthened its position on the airfield and beat back all German counter-attacks, but the British effort to bring up forces from the south via Gabr Saleh and have them close up on the area of the airfield was not only difficult but also cost precious time. In any case, concentrated afternoon attacks by Stukas and ME-110 Zerstörers in support of German attacks near Sidi Rezegh helped weaken British positions up to the heights on the airfield southern edge.

On the British XIII Corps front, units of the 4th Indian Division advanced from the east and south on the German–Italian positions from Halfaya Pass to Sidi Omar. At the same time, troops of the 2nd New Zealand Division came up from the west towards the same objectives. Clashes of varying intensity resulted. In the process, the somewhat hesitant advance of the New Zealanders was affected by the probes of the *DAK* coming from the west. By evening, the New Zealanders' divisional staff and artillery were still west of Sidi Omar. Consequently, the hoped-for forward movement by British forces to the north with the object of breaking through west of Capuzzo and Bardia had not yet entered a decisive stage.

On the whole, the situation's lack of clarity for German commanders on 20 November led essentially to a lost day, a faulty employment of their armoured formations and a limited success. Almost involuntarily, the British Eighth Army used the situation to good effect and strengthened its position near Sidi Rezegh. It also brought together other armoured brigades. For its part, XIII Corps saw itself in a good initial position to take advantage of a possible link-up with the garrison at Tobruk to the north if XXX Corps managed definitively to fix the German armoured forces in place. Nonetheless, British commanders were by no means confident. They knew that German forces were prepared to act, but they also knew that the situation could not be adequately assessed. British commanders had established no operational point of main effort (*Schwerpunkt*). Instead, they had employed major formations in more-or-less preconceived actions between Sollum and Bir el Gubi and scattered those formations widely. They were fortunate that the German armoured forces missed the chance to throw themselves on the most threatening of the British formations in the area Gabr Saleh–Sidi Rezegh.

B. The *Afrika Korps* Accepts Battle

Only on the night of 20 November did Rommel and his staff come to see that the action was not merely an attempt to relieve Tobruk but rather that everything since 18 November indicated a British offensive. Not least, British radio was confirming German suspicions since it was reporting in news broadcasts a general offensive by Eighth Army, including the offensive's direction and the army's strength. This forced the *Panzergruppe* to deploy its armoured formations *en masse*. Given numerical inferiority on the German side, the effort would be made to overwhelm British formations individually and defeat them in detail. Consequently, that night *Panzergruppe Afrika* sent the following order to the *DAK*: 'On 21 November, from the area approximately 25km west of Sidi Omar, attack the rear of the enemy advancing on Tobruk in the direction of Bel Hamed.' This order was followed by one at 0400 hours stressing the urgency of the situation: 'Move as rapidly as possible.' At the same time, the British 7th Armoured Brigade and 7th Support Group had established a combined combat-command so as to create conditions for an attack towards Tobruk on 21 November in combination with a breakout attempt by the beleaguered fortress' garrison.

Thus, on the morning of 21 November, the Division *zbV Afrika* found itself in action near Sidi Rezegh against a British 7th Armoured Brigade once again advancing on Tobruk. And once again, the Germans held firm. In their rear, the Italian 25th Infantry Division *Bologna*, along with German reinforcements, prevented a breakout on the south-east of the ring encircling Tobruk by troops inside the city. In the face of repeated attacks in the first half of the day, deep penetrations could not be prevented. These, however, were partially won back during the day. Nonetheless, the reinforced 3rd Panzer Reconnaissance Detachment had to be called in during the afternoon. Axis forces thereby recovered several positions which had been lost around 1100 hours in an effort at a breakout supported by some 50 tanks, numerous British vehicles being lost in this action. By nightfall, the situation of the *Bologna* division and its sister, the 17th Infantry Division *Pavia*, had been generally restored, but both had suffered losses of personnel, materiel (eight batteries of guns) and ground.

On the morning of 21 November, a dully cool and rainy day, the *DAK* broke contact with the British 4th and 22nd Brigades. A rearguard, fronted to the south and south-east and reinforced with anti-tank and anti-aircraft guns, was established to prevent an advance of these formations. The Germans managed to avoid serious mechanical shortfalls and thereby prevented any hindering of the attack. At midday that day, however, the two sides lost contact, as the British formations had to refuel.

The mass of the German armoured divisions now attacked on a broad front to the north-west: on the right, 21st Panzer Division in the direction of Bel Hamed; on the left, 15th Panzer Division towards Sidi Rezegh by way of Sidi Muftan. In an attack off the march, and with accompanying artillery close alongside, they drove back strong enemy armoured formations of perhaps 100 British tanks early on. By midday they had been pushed south-east of Sidi Rezegh to the heights of the escarpment beyond. The commander of the British 7th Armoured Brigade had ceased his own attack toward the north-west and in response threw the bulk of his armour against the Germans. The actual defence of the airfield was left principally to the Support Group. In the process, the *Afrika Korps* clashed to the south-west with British anti-tank guns and field artillery, even as British tanks launched a flanking attack. Until nightfall, hard-fought, mobile battles repeatedly erupted with losses on both sides (for the British some 30 tanks), but German forces failed to take the airfield. Though the British were caught up in a swirling battle throughout, they managed to survive, especially the crisis of the middle of the day. Further, after a pause to refuel and resupply, the British 4th and 22nd Armoured Brigades moved dangerously against the logistics elements and south-west flanks of the German armoured divisions. The combatants separated only with the onset of darkness. North of Sidi Muftan, 15th Panzer Division thereafter went over to a defensive hedgehog position, and 21st Panzer did the same south of Point 175. That same night, however, 15th Panzer was ordered to begin moving to the area south of Gambut; 21st Panzer followed suit but to the south of Safran.

During the same day, thrusts by the 1st South African Division – which had arrived in the meantime – had been neatly repulsed along the front of the Italian Corps *Gambara* near Bir el Gubi. As a precaution, Italian commander General Gastone Gambara had moved elements of the 101st Motorised Division *Trieste* from Bir Hakim forward and to the east. Further to the west, enemy motorised units, with their accompanying armoured reconnaissance vehicles, were discovered already on the march in a westerly direction near Ben Genia. These were fiercely attacked by the *Luftwaffe*.

Somewhat by contrast, relative calm prevailed on the Sollum front. While the British 4th Indian Division secured the encirclement from the south-east, the 2nd New Zealand Division was deployed moving north around midday with more than 100 'I' (Infantry) tanks of the 1st Army Armoured Brigade to the west of Axis positions. Their objective was to push across the Trigh Capuzzo to Sidi Rezegh and on to Tobruk. It remains unclear whether merely a timetable had been established to execute a preconceived plan or whether this objective was newly developed from the situation at that hour. The inspiration seems to have grown out of the fact that the command posts of the British 7th Armoured Division and XXX Corps, which lay far to the rear, underestimated the fighting strength of the *DAK* and judged it to be worn out on the night of 20 November. Further, those command centres took to heart the assessment of the 4th and 22nd Brigades that Rommel's armoured formations were withdrawing to the north-west. Consequently, they believed that Rommel already saw the battle as lost. General Auchinleck shared this assessment and issued orders accordingly. He thereby managed to secure the area on both sides of Sidi Aziz by the 2nd New Zealand Division without fighting, as well as occupying the outer districts of Bardia and Capuzzo. Even Rommel was forced to transfer his headquarters from the endangered area near Gambut during the night of 21–22 November to El Adem. In this way, the British decision became one of the keys to success. On the British side, only the 7th Armoured Division had found itself actively engaged to that point. Now it could concentrate in a fashion that had eluded it thus far. In addition, other offensive formations of Eighth Army had pushed forward into the broad space between Sidi Omar and Bir el Gubi.

Still, on the night of 21 November, *Panzergruppe Afrika* did not see itself in a difficult situation. A link-up between enemy formations south-east of Tobruk and the fortress itself had been prevented. The *DAK* had executed a successful attack of its own and stood poised in a key position between the enemy's armoured brigades with a remaining possibility of defeating each of them in detail. Meanwhile, the British XIII Corps remained stuck far to the east of its initial position. Nevertheless, there was no time to lose. Unfortunately for the Axis forces, German air support had been insufficient, and British strength was estimated – indeed overestimated – to be as many as 300 tanks.

In this situation, supply conditions on the German side, and their effects on decision-making, were not immaterial. The *Afrika Korps* had already complained of insufficient armour-piercing ammunition during the day, especially for use against the gun-shields of anti-tank guns and field artillery pieces. That night fuel shortages added to the *DAK*'s woes. Available fuel aboard the vehicles and in the armoured formations' reserves sufficed only for a general movement to the area of Safran–Gambut. In light of this situation, combined with a still-threatened link-up of the garrison inside Tobruk with the British 7th Armoured Division, Rommel's orders for 22 November specified defensive operations, including the incorporation of the Special Duty Division *Afrika*. The assessments of the *DAK*'s commander were also no doubt influenced by the fact that, until enough fuel and ammunition were on hand, offensive action on 22 November was impossible. He did not want to leave them stranded in the enemy's midst as long as they were only partially mobile. Consequently, he did not follow the recommendations of the commander of 15th Panzer Division (General Walter Neumann-Silkow), who had accurately assessed both the enemy's intentions and his own (15th Panzer's) favourable tactical situation and had therefore urged a continuation of the attack. General Ludwig Crüwell wanted to assemble his forces to the north–east and lead the *DAK* in a flank attack against the British. If a move onto the defensive then became necessary, the breadth of the operational space would itself help ensure the success of such an action.

Rommel's orders to the *DAK* for 22 November, however, indicated that it was to hold the area already taken and prevent the enemy armoured formations facing it from linking up with the garrison in Tobruk. Simultaneously, he reckoned on beginning attacks against the front and rear of the Sollum–Bardia line. The *DAK* received these orders at 2240 hours but, astonishingly, did no more than follow the part which stated 'reposition units to the north-east during the night'. Consequently, on the morning of 22 November, only the rearguard encountered the enemy. The 15th Panzer Division shifted south of Gambut, and 21st Panzer, coming down scot-free from the escarpment, reached the area of Bel Hamed–Safran to the north of the Trigh Capuzzo. In this way, the *DAK* believed that it had best met its instructions. Insofar as operational freedom was concerned, that was correct. In the process, however, the favourability of the tactical situation was ignored.

German supply columns reached the deployed forces only during the first half of the day. The *DAK*'s fighting movements over the preceding three days not only hindered the logistics elements' efforts to locate the combat units, but also exhausted those supplies which had been collected east of Tobruk in the latter's immediate vicinity. It now became necessary to draw ammunition and fuel from the *Panzergruppe's* dumps south-west of Tobruk. The increasingly lengthened supply lines, combined with uncertainty and the narrowness of road passage near El Duda and Sidi Rezegh, resulted not only in lost time but also influenced commanders' assessments of the general situation on the night of 21 November. By contrast, the British 7th Armoured Division was able to use the moment to bring up the 22nd and 4th Brigades to the area around the airfield. In addition, the reinforced 5th South African (SA) Brigade – the foremost combat element of the 1st SA Division – was moved from Bir el Gobi to attack the southern flank of the Germans' 155th Rifle Regiment near Point 178.

Thus, while the *DAK* seemed to be favourably positioned to continue the fight for the airfield, in fact the advantage lay with the British XXX Corps. Both sides spent the morning disposing and resupplying their forces. Meanwhile, the *DAK* rearguard's efforts to hold off the British led to contact being lost entirely with the enemy's following forces, and breakout attempts from Tobruk itself were halted by German artillery fire. The *Afrika* Division held off advances of the British 7th Armoured Division while their German counterparts refuelled. The 1st SA Division slowly occupied the zone from Bir el Gobi northward. For its part, the British XIII Corps launched an attack on the Sollum front near Sidi Omar, but without success; Capuzzo, however, as it appeared to be unoccupied, was taken. Rommel had nothing with which to oppose this corps. He was consequently forced to attack, first, the British armour and then the remaining elements. Against the 2nd New Zealand (NZ) Corps he could deploy only reconnaissance forces.

In seizing the initiative once more, Rommel was particularly influenced by the morning's favourable reports from the units ringing Tobruk; by similar reports from Sidi Rezegh; and those regarding the *DAK's* supply situation. At midday on 22 November, he personally scheduled an attack by the now rested and mission-capable 21st Panzer Division against the enemy at Sidi Rezegh. While the mechanised infantry advanced from the north supported by the bulk of the artillery and elements of the Division *zbV Afrika*, a reinforced 5th Panzer Regiment marched across the roadway near El Duda and reached the area west of the airfield. From here the German armour formed up to the east. Intending to destroy the British 7th Armoured Division, this German pincer attack caught the approximately 180 British tanks in the area by surprise, leading to a battle the latter accepted. Accompanied throughout by intense fire from artillery and flak guns, the engagement grew rapidly and became a major contest for Sidi Rezegh and the airfield. Fallen soldiers and burning vehicles littered the smoke- and dust-shrouded battlefield. That same afternoon, the British 7th Support Group was forced to abandon the airfield it had occupied for three days. With the 7th Brigade, the Support Group re-established itself further to the south. Preparing to counter–attack from the south, the British 22nd Brigade was in turn hit in front and on the flank. The Germans broke through the brigade in the growing darkness, and during the fighting destroyed some 45 of the brigade's 79 tanks. The rest were scattered. That night, and by then possessing only limited combat capability, 22nd Brigade withdrew with other units of the 7th Armoured Division. This withdrawal left the airfield to 21st Panzer Division, along with control of the escarpment and POWs. Meanwhile, the attack on the south-west wing by the 5th SA Brigade had brought neither success nor relief.

Further eastward, Crüwell, the commanding general of the *DAK*, also undertook to move 15th Panzer Division from the area of Sciaf towards the eastern flank of the British 7th Armoured Division but without having been able to coordinate his intentions with Rommel. Moving late in the afternoon, 15th Panzer initially had little contact with the enemy. At dusk, however, and while advancing in open order, the Germans suddenly encountered and completely surprised formations of British tanks and other vehicles. As burning British machines lit up the darkness, the Germans' coup succeeded completely. They had managed to overrun the command post of the British 4th Brigade, as well as the tanks and vehicles of the 8th Hussar Regiment. All of the these were either destroyed, captured or scattered. British losses amounted to some 35 tanks, plus all remaining armoured vehicles, guns and communications gear.

The *DAK* thus scored an enormous victory on 22 November. Significant elements of the British 7th Armoured Division, including about half of its tanks, were destroyed. The 4th Armoured Brigade had essentially ceased to exist, and 22nd Armoured Brigade was badly ground down. Furthermore, the airfield was in German hands; breakout attempts from Tobruk had been turned back; and the reinforced 29th Indian Regiment had been decimated by aerial attacks far to the west and fixed in place. Only the British XXX Corps had managed to exploits its freedom of movement to seize strongpoints along the Sollum front. In addition, supported by the 6th NZ Brigade, it had pushed west along the route of the desert tracks. To try to thwart this movement, the Germans had been able to employ only the 3rd Armoured Reconnaissance Battalion along the Via Balbia and the 33rd Armoured Reconnaissance Battalion along the Trigh Capuzzo.

For the four days' fighting, *Panzergruppe Afrika* reported the destruction of 207 British tanks, and a further 50 tanks and 200 armoured vehicles destroyed by the Italian Corps *Gambarra*. British sources noted that the 453 tanks of the 7th Armoured Division were reduced to 150. General Auchinleck reported on 23 November that the 7th Brigade possessed only 10 tanks ready for action and the 22nd Brigade about 40. Additionally, there were a number of tanks available from the 4th Brigade's 3rd Royal Tank Regiment in the area south of Sidi Rezegh. Darkness made the disentangling of the British forces south-east of Tobruk difficult, but the various elements of the *DAK* managed to sort themselves out. On the escarpment, south of Sidi Rezegh, 21st Panzer Division set itself up defensively on a broad front, keeping mobile offensive reserves ready on the flanks. At the same time, 15th Panzer Division collected itself in a readiness position south-west of Sciaf-Sciuf.

C. The Armoured Battle and Operational Movements

General Rommel's intention remained the destruction of British forces south of Sidi Rezegh. Though gaining an overview of events, he could no longer issue orders in person and in a timely fashion. Consequently, beginning at 2230 hours, he sent out mission orders for 23 November via radio.

(Excerpt):

'1. ...

2. On 23 November, the *Panzergruppe* will force a decision south-east of Tobruk through concentric attacks by the *DAK* and elements of Corps *Gambarra*. Corps *Gambarra* to attack with elements of the *Ariete* Armoured Division at 0800 hours from el Gubi in the direction of Gambut.

3. On 23 November, *DAK* to move at 0700 hours in the general direction of Bir el Gubi. Strict concentration of force will be maintained with the point of main effort [*Schwerpunkt*] on the left flank. The enemy will be encircled and destroyed. The centre line of advance and the thrust line [*Stoßlinie*] is Hill 176 – Bir el Gubi (Map: 1:100,000) (6km south-east of Sidi Rezegh). Thrust line begins at Hill 176, number 30. Recognition signal for German and Italian forces will be the firing of two white flares. *DAK* troops to be informed that the *Ariete* Division is using, in part, captured British vehicles. Resupply route is to run by way of Sidi Rezegh. Corps command post – in the area of Bel Hamed – is to report.

4. ...'

The order did not reach the *DAK*'s commander in time. He nevertheless correctly situated his troops in keeping with Rommel's intent. Using principally infantry and artillery, 21st Panzer Division was to hold off all enemy attacks in the direction of Tobruk. Meanwhile, 15th Panzer Division would attack in the direction of Bir el Gubi while keeping its main effort on the left flank. It would link up with the *Ariete* Armoured Division advancing from Bir el Gubi, encircle British forces from the south and begin their annihilation. To this end, 5th Panzer Regiment was attached. To the west and north, respectively, the Italian divisions *Trieste* and *Pavia* would stand on the defensive between Bir el Gubi and El Adem, with their front facing east. Serving as the army's reserve would be the 155th Rifle Regiment and the 261st *Afrika* Regiment. They occupied positions that were partially included in 21st Panzer's operational area and partially in the 'quiet' western front of Sidi Rezegh. As these preparations were underway, on the night of 22–23 November, Mussolini ordered that all Italian troops in the region of Marmarica would now fall under Rommel's command, a decision that doubtless made German–Italian strength more effectively unified. This decision from Rome also included the Corps *Gambarra*, now serving as additional reserve.

Meanwhile, the British were also arranging their forces. They still preserved a substantial fighting force on the battlefield, especially regarding anti-tank guns and artillery. In addition, the 5th SA Brigade began to arrive overnight as the leading element of the 1st SA Division. In the east, XIII Corps prepared its attack, advancing the 6th NZ Brigade during the night in the direction of Tobruk. At about 0600 hours the brigade's forward units surprised the *DAK*'s command post near Gasr el Arid. They made valuable prisoners of the corps' operations and intelligence officers and staff-personnel. They also captured several communications vehicles. Luckily for the Germans, the *DAK*'s commanding general and his chief of staff had left only half an hour before, headed for 15th Panzer Division.

The Decisive Engagement

The World War I commemorative day on the German calendar, Sunday of the Dead – 23 November – dawned with thick ground fog. Hardly had the fog begun to lift, at about 0700 hours, than the reinforced 15th Panzer Division began to move. While certain of its elements had to climb the escarpment, further to the west the *Afrika* Regiment relieved units of the 15th Rifle Brigade from their defensive positions. Nevertheless, the planned attack-formations could not be assumed since the 5th Panzer Regiment hadn't appeared on time and had subsequently to follow up to the right rear. Further, an artillery detachment had to be left behind to support the *Afrika* Regiment.

Soon, however, 8th Panzer Regiment made contact with enemy tanks and other vehicles. It swung momentarily to the south and drove the enemy to flight. Following on in the second echelon, the rifle brigade halted and held off British armour's flanking attacks with anti-tank guns. Enemy forces repeatedly appeared in front, on the flanks and to the rear, and their artillery fire pounded the division constantly from the west, south and north-west. But the German armoured drive – typical for an attack against the flanks and rear of the enemy – broke over the British supply troops and their protective screen. In the process, the German armour later engaged the 7th Support Group. Luckily for the British, the German armour also unintentionally made contact with the 3rd RTR and drew it into the fight as the latter proceeded to the rest area of the 4th Brigade which lay to the south. The German attack thus hit a number of British formations and either drove them back, scattered them or broke through them. Across a broad front, British forces were easy prey for German tanks and artillery, but not without loss for the attackers. In the middle of the battle, the tank-destroyer brigade following on the right rear as protection for the attackers' deep flank had to be ordered to shift all the way to the left front due to reported threats of enemy armour from the south-east. Characteristic of the fighting were repeated eruptions of heavy fire of all arms in the deep eastern flank of the British main forces and the running battles of movement in the area around Sidi Muftan and to the south-west. These forced the Germans to fight battles of fire and movement that were both broad and deep. Groups of enemy troops repeatedly appeared everywhere. This phase of the fighting consequently inflicted heavy attrition on both sides' forces, and especially large loss of vehicles on the British side.

Initially, British forces were surprised by the German drive, but the Germans were struck both by British troops' numbers and their tenacity. Once again, 7th Support Group's commander, General Campbell, succeeded in rapidly building up blocking positions employing tanks, anti-tank guns and artillery around Bir el Halad, and thus in the British pocket, with fronts facing south and south-east. Constant and heavy artillery support saved the British forces from complete destruction, even though the Germans repeatedly scattered British supply columns and engaged the rear-guard of the 5th and the advance guard of 1st SA Brigades on the flanks, breaking through the formations and forcing them to fight. In the meantime, due to repeated halts, firefights, pursuits and rearrangements, the bulk of 15th Panzer Division resumed its drive in the direction of Bir el Gubi only after 1050 hours. Here, too, the division was continuously harassed by artillery fire. Diverting around a swampy area, it linked up with the *Ariete* Division about 12km north-east of Bir el Gubi at 1235 hours, thus completing the enclosing manoeuvre toward the south-west.

After regrouping and undertaking another approach march, General Crüwell started his main drive at 1500 hours, this time from the south and on a broad front employing all available forces. Attacking northward, his formations were arranged in such a way as to push the enemy up against the defensive front of 21st Panzer Division and thereby annihilate them. The 15th Panzer Division thereby doubled back with 5th Panzer Regiment on the right, while on the left marched 8th Panzer Regiment, reinforced with artillery and flak guns. The former was followed by the rifle brigade, supported by the 1st Battalion, 18th Flak Regiment, and Regiment *zbV 200*, while the latter had the 115th Rifle Regiment behind. Cooperating with each of the rifle regiments were separate detachments from the 33rd Artillery Regiment. The *Ariete* Division was assigned to the left but came up late; it was therefore only involved on the fringes of the fighting.

Intending to attack rapidly and in as concentrated a fashion as possible, with the objective of breaking into and through the enemy formations with the infantry following close behind, the Germans nevertheless found themselves expected. Effectively harassed by artillery even as they assembled, the Germans encountered ever heavier fire from both artillery and anti-tank guns as they advanced in the attempt to overrun the British field positions and get in among their supporting elements. The attack ran into prepared defences and fire from weapons of all calibres. Already-heavy British artillery fire increased in intensity. Troops of the 5th SA Brigade fought bravely, letting German tanks and mechanised infantry get close enough to destroy them in hand-to-hand combat. In this, they were ably supported by flanking fire from anti-tank guns. The Germans could break through only in the central sector, and then only as a result of combined-arms and directly supporting efforts. The 115th Rifle Regiment was quickly ordered to that sector, but the mounted infantrymen could not widen the breach that had been made by the armour. In repeated assaults, now partly dismounted, nearly all commanders and crews, along with their infantry fighting vehicles, were shot down, and it was only after reassembling that the regiment could resume its attack. Meanwhile, neighbouring armoured detachments, ably shown the way by the 1st Battalion, 8th Panzer Regiment, managed to move forward in the breach. In the process, the battle dissolved into countless individual tank duels, firefights of all calibres, and infantry attacks and counter-attacks. A south-east flanking drive on the left by the British 22nd Brigade reignited the fighting but without being able to force a decision. Finally, at about 1700 hours, 1st Battalion, 8th Panzer Regiment, linked up with 21st Panzer Division on the airfield after managing to fight its way on the middle-right sector of the front through enemy positions some 10km deep, thus deciding the day, even though the fighting continued with no less intensity. Moving eastward to avoid heavy enemy defensive fire, despite resistance, 5th Panzer Regiment also succeeded in linking up with 21st Panzer Division's eastern flank, while the 2nd Battalion, 8th Panzer Regiment, subdued the defensive resistance of enemy tanks, mobile artillery and infantry on the left of the breach. That success, however, required repeated assaults and heavy losses.

About 1730 hours, the British defence, including artillery fire, subsided along the entire front, though the broad plain south of Sidi Rezegh remained enveloped in the fire, dense smoke and noise resulting from a massive armoured and artillery battle. In many places, bitter fighting extended past dusk. Numerous tanks, heavy weapons and vehicles from both sides were lost, burnt out or broken down. Losses were heavy. As visibility decreased even before the onset of darkness, individual English [sic] vehicles and guns evaded the German assault columns and wolf packs of tanks to break out of the encirclement, and the battle, and drive south. The broad mass, however, remained essentially surrounded by German forces as night fell.

Only after the onset of darkness did the battle slowly die down. Total losses, prisoners and captured matériel still couldn't be completely accounted for by midnight. The total scale of losses remained incomplete to the staff of *Panzergruppe Afrika* for days. Friendly and enemy troops – scattered, exhausted, surprised, wounded, fleeing, sleeping and even still fighting – were encountered for days afterward in the wider region of the battle. While the British had managed to prevent the complete destruction of 7th Armoured Division, the Germans had scored a clear tactical success. No commanders spoke of actual victory.

German commanders had evidently not initially reckoned with so many British formations being between Sidi Rezegh and Bir el Gubi. They undoubtedly did not fully exploit the success of the surprising of enemy troops that morning near Sidi Muftan. An immediate attack to the west at that place that morning may well have led to a penetration of the centre of the British positions south of the airfield at Sidi Rezegh and, in all likelihood, to the destruction of the larger portion of the enemy forces, possibly also avoiding the Germans' own heavy losses. In any case, the available German assault forces (i.e. 15th Panzer Division) were too few to encircle all the British forces in an area stretching to the south to a distance of 15—20 km between Sidi Muftan and Bir el Gubi. Then, too, every passing hour decreased the value of the German surprise and increased that of the British defence.

With the coming of night, the two opponents separated. The overnight task for the Germans was to reassemble, resupply and establish close security. For the British, the watchwords were the collection of combat-capable forces to the south and south-east; collection in the rear of baggage trains striving to drive out of the combat zone; and the reconstitution of fleeing elements. Reports of war correspondents who experienced the fighting on the British side indicate that jeeps, trucks and stray crews took days to find their way back to their units.

Even as the fighting abated, 15th Panzer Division began to establish rear-area security in the south-east. The division ordered the 33rd Armoured Reconnaissance Detachment to oversee force-protection and resupply for the German units during the night west and north of Sidi Muftan. The same unit was to undertake forward reconnaissance at daybreak. Noteworthy here is the area stretching from Bel Hamed in the north-north-west to Sidi Muftan far to the south-east. Was the enemy still present? Could the path of his withdrawal be determined? And was he still in the surrounding area?

The troops of the *DAK* were fought out. Understandably, they wanted and needed rest. It took a significant portion of the night to reassemble the various units in any case. Fuel tanks were largely empty, and the mass of available ammunition had been expended. Supply columns had held back due to uncertainty concerning the German forces' operational area on 23 November, as well as to the fighting's outcome and the columns' ability to find the units in question. Even at the onset of darkness, logistics elements still had neither a general awareness of where they were supposed to be nor actual contact with the combat troops. Only at about 2200 hours did radio requests go out for resupply. They were to come by the shortest possible route from the west or north, via Sidi Rezegh. They were to climb the escarpment and were expected before dawn. The most urgent needs included ambulances to evacuate the wounded, but also water, fuel and ammunition, especially for the armour and field howitzers. But even though commanders demanded resupply before daybreak, it did not occur due to miscalculation of the time-to-travel requirements for the logistics units and other complications. In fact, most of the supply columns reached the combat units only during the first half of the morning of 24 November. The recovery of damaged tanks and their repair either on site or at the maintenance companies' areas also went well into the day, and only as a result of redoubled effort.

The dependence of armoured units on effective means of command showed clearly in these instances. The surprise attack on the *DAK*'s command post, the losses during the day and joint battle all showed the inadequacies of radio communications. Furthermore, until the arrival of new codes and encryption devices during the morning, radio silence reigned. Of course, this necessity didn't make resupply or the establishment of a new order of battle any easier. It thus becomes understandable that 21st Panzer Division wasn't mission-capable until about 0900 hours on 24 November, and 15th Panzer Division not until noon.

Subsidiary Fighting

On the periphery of this battle occurred others that helped shape the operational situation for the following days. While the 1st SA Brigade remained outside the battle area, the 6th NZ Brigade continued its westward advance in the north-eastern sector of the battlefield. Its pressure was felt near Point 175 during the course of the day. Nevertheless, *Afrika* Regiment 361 was able to maintain its positions on the eastern edge of the airfield, with its own front now also facing east. Evidently, Rommel himself appears to have become stuck there in his effort to follow 15th

Panzer Division's advance. Only in the evening was he able to get out and return to his headquarters near El Adem. In the meantime, elements of the 2nd NZ Division had taken Gambut. The bulk of that division subsequently followed westward, while leaving some units behind and deployed at Bardia. Other formations of the British XIII Corps were also active. At numerous points near Sollum and Halfaya Pass, units went over to the attack. German forces, however, managed to repel all those attacks, even though most were supported by armour. The British succeeded only in capturing Upper Sollum.

In the day's somewhat less intense fighting in the south-eastern sector of the ring around Tobruk, the British garrison had managed to overrun a German position in an armour–supported assault. Meanwhile, 21st Panzer Division (minus 5th Panzer Regiment) did its part on the northern wing of the battles around Sidi Rezegh. Through effective fire, manoeuvre and defence, the division prevented a link-up of the besieged garrison and elements of the British XXX Corps. Further, according to Italian reports, the already decimated battle group consisting of the remnants of the 29th Indian Regiment reached the oasis of Gialo. They played no major part in the fighting thereafter.

The High Point

The day resulted in a clear tactical success for the Germans south-east of Tobruk. In addition, there was the presumed success in warding off the immediate threat to the Axis forces encircling the city and the destruction of the mass of the attacking British armoured forces. On the other hand, however, the strategic advantage lay with the British. They'd seized the initiative in the border area of Sollum. They'd prevented decisive losses to XXX Corps' attacking formations. And they'd improved the prospects for a raising of the siege of Tobruk. But as for actual losses from this battle of the Sunday of the Dead, there will likely never be total clarity. The commanders themselves did not know. The situation on 24 November forced them once again into the fight before they could establish the tallies.

The German rifle regiments suffered significant losses, especially regarding commanders, officers and NCOs. In the two armoured regiments, approximately 70 of the 150 tanks which started the battle were out of action, about 20 having been destroyed. The *DAK* possessed barely 80 operational tanks on the morning of 24 November, though it also captured weapons and equipment and had taken more than 2,000 POWs. The general situation is illustrated by a report from the 8th Panzer Regiment on the evening of the 23rd:

	Pz II	Pz III	Pz IV	Lg. Bef. **[drivable?]** Vehicles	Sm. Bef. **[drivable?]** Vehicles
Operational	18	36	7	3	1
Losses	14	30	9	1	1
No. losses written off	6	10	3	---	---

British losses were also heavy. They, too, lost some 70 tanks and many artillery pieces, self-propelled gun carriages and motor vehicles. There were even reports of more than 100 tanks lost. The 5th SA Brigade was nearly annihilated, 22nd Brigade was hard hit and many other units were scattered. These subsequently attempted to regroup on either side of the Trigh el Abd. In the process, Gaber Saleh and other surrounding spots, including command posts and supply dumps, were turned into strongpoints. Indeed, the morning of 24 November even revealed that significant British and South African forces had escaped the pocket under the cover of darkness. Still, it remained that in some cases it took days for resupply troops and individual vehicles and crews to reach their respective parent units, and not without further adventures in the desert.

The battle now reached its high point. Heavy attrition of armoured and infantry units had been accompanied by losses of officers and other leaders. The decisive combat units on both sides now more than ever had to rely upon their inherent ability to reconstitute themselves effectively. Here the British brigades enjoyed the advantage. Their possession of a larger effective personnel-strength and deeper matériel reserves proved in the long run of greater value than the Germans' ability to improvise and rapidly raise the level of their operational strength. Then too, British reserves had not yet been committed. Furthermore, British airpower inflicted significant damage whenever the two sides were not commingled on the battlefield. By contrast, German and Italian aircraft appeared ever less frequently.

The commander of the British Eighth Army, now headquartered at Maddalena, saw his own position in grim terms. The now evident destruction of his armoured forces – and thereby his attacking strength – in combination with the disappointing results in front of Tobruk and Sollum, led General Cunningham to determine that a continuation of his offensive would not promise success. His thoughts thus turned to possibly breaking off the battle and regrouping his forces on Egyptian territory. By contrast, General Auchinleck, on the scene as he was, did not see the admittedly serious situation in so hopeless a light. He believed that he saw more clearly the likely balance of forces with Rommel, and the latter's not exactly rosy situation, on 23 November. Auchinleck prevailed. The fighting would continue.

The German Drive Into the Strategic Depth

Heretofore, Rommel did not experience the battle first-hand. Only late that night did he learn from General Crüwell's reports about the battle's course that the English [sic] armoured forces had been destroyed, as well as the larger situation in the whole of Cyrenaica. He certainly did not – and could not – know about the cost to Axis forces in achieving these results. He was likewise unaware not only of the full extent of the 2nd NZ Division's threatening movements near Gambut and further to the west, but also the preparations being made for another breakout attempt by the garrison in Tobruk. Furthermore, he evidently overestimated the extent of the defeat of British forces around Sidi Rezegh, since he did not know precisely which enemy troops had been involved in the fighting.

Consequently, he thought that the British 7th Armoured Division had been literally destroyed. Rommel evidently took this assessment into account in making his decision to pursue the remaining enemy forces, particularly in that it encompassed an attack upon the dangerous threat posed by the enemy near Sollum. His successes therefore encouraged him to lay his point of main effort in a drive into the strategic depth of the British Eighth Army and combine that drive with support for Axis forces in area of Sollum and Halfaya Pass. He trusted in his weakened units to complete the destruction of the enemy whom he supposed encircled south-east of Sidi Rezegh. In this phase, Rommel also evidently overestimated the strategic value of reports from his own isolated units near the border regarding the enemy's situation, as he did the sensitivity of the British rear.

Thus, he determined during the night of 23–24 November to advance in the direction of Sidi Omar and attack the enemy on the Sollum front, but he did so without first completing the destruction of the British 7th Armoured Division. At the same time, he was able to overtake British forces which had escaped the pocket, as well as establish contact with British elements at the rear of the main body. Behind the front encircling Tobruk, he established a battle group on either side of Bel Hamed under *Generalmajor* Böttcher (Artillery Command 104) consisting of two battalions of the 155th Rifle Regiment, one battalion of the 361st *Afrika* Regiment, the 900th Combat Engineer (*Pioneer*) Battalion and elements of the army's artillery. On the left, the Division *zbV Afrika* was tasked with defending on both sides of the Via Balbia against possible attacks from the east and any breakout attempt from the west. Even as these preparations were under way at sunrise on 24 November, units of the British XXX Corps were attempting to regroup and order themselves in the area between Gambut and Gabr Saleh. In addition, 1st SA Brigade was falling back as ordered to cover the western flank between Bir el Gubi and Gabr Saleh.

The fighting on the preceding day's battlefield did not resume. Rommel hardly gave the *DAK* time for the necessary resupply. Accompanied by his chief of staff and a small command staff, he left his headquarters, placed himself at the head of 21st Panzer Division and got under way in the direction of Sidi Omar at 1000 hours. He was followed by 15th Panzer Division at 1230 hours. The *Ariete* Division began to move at about 1300 hours and maintained position directly to the right rear. Advancing rapidly and deeply over a wide area, and without halting on the flanks, the battle groups drove through and scattered British units and vehicle parks wherever they found them in the desert. German troops hardly fought. More often, they simply encountered rear-area British elements or already-scattered columns.

The two German armoured divisions advanced in echelon. In the process, 15th Panzer Division swapped its reconnaissance detachment for other units in the left rear so as to intervene more quickly should fighting to the north-east require it. The enemy parallelled the *DAK* on both flanks and kept up noticeable artillery fire. However, actual attacks by British tanks – these were perhaps scattered units trying to move from north-east to south-west – were repulsed at great range by the Germans' own field artillery and flak guns used in the anti-tank role.

Panic, alarm and a desire to flee now seized the enemy far to the south-east of the preceding day's battlefield. More than a few crews, whose vehicles had escaped the earlier fighting on the airfield, lost their nerve when they now encountered the pursuing Germans and slew their compasses to the south–east to avoid destruction. Most halted only when they reached various command posts along the Trigh el Abd and some – as reported in certain eyewitness accounts – not until they'd actually gained the frontier wire, strung years before by the Italians along the Egyptian border.

The area between Gambut, Bardia, Sidi Omar and Gaber Saleh dissolved in confusion. The German attack to the south-east continued by way of Bir el Chelb and Bir el Melia. In short order, the *DAK* crashed into trailing elements of the 4th Indian Division west of Sidi Omar and in the afternoon reached the Libyan–Egyptian border to the south. While the mass of 21st Panzer Division pushed on across the wire headed east, 5th Panzer Regiment remained west of the wire and to the south of the Trigh el Abd. As night fell, the division's various elements took up protective 'hedgehog' positions.

On the same day, Sidi Omar was taken by the 7th Indian Brigade, almost the sole victory of the Indian division. That said, however, less than half of the division's strength was committed. The 11th Indian Brigade was held back around the high ground near Buq-Buq, and the 5th Indian Brigade was assigned protection of the railhead of the British supply line at Sofafi. By contrast, British fliers now found rich hunting in the desert and, for the first time, inflicted painful losses on the *DAK*.

For example, aerial attacks destroyed the 33rd Armoured Reconnaissance Detachment's last operational armoured recce vehicle. Consequently, the *DAK* was dispersed widely and in great depth as night fell. As the darkness initially came on, 15th Panzer Division stopped to refuel and in the process lost contact with units of the 21st Panzer Division. In the dark, seeking to re-establish that contact, 15th Panzer Division collided with British tanks and was caught up in a brief engagement. This forced the division to go into a 'hedgehog' position at 2200 hours approximately 25km south-west of Sidi Omar. Nevertheless, the infantry continued to move up along the Trigh el Abd and approached the border zone. This allowed contact to be made with 5th Panzer Regiment and simultaneously helped secure that unit. The Italian *Ariete* Division did not move much at all to the east beyond the area it already occupied north of Gabr Saleh.

An important event occurring on this day was the fact that the *DAK* bypassed several – in part unguarded – British supply dumps in the desert. Remarkably, combat elements went into prepared positions or operational areas without disturbing them. An explanation is hard to come by: it remains the case that either the German armoured commanders knew of the dumps but assigned them too little significance, or did not actually know about them. It is certainly true that those commanders had too few reconnaissance assets at their disposal. In any case, the British were to remain in control of their substantial sources of fuel and ammunition, ones that were very close to the front.

The German drive once again created disorder among the staffs and troops of the Eighth Army. Even the army's main headquarters at Maddalena packed up in a hurry. General Cunningham deemed the situation just as catastrophic as the day before. He no longer trusted a plan of attack whose trump card – the tanks of 7th Armoured Division – had lost its sting. Once again, he saw his own estimate of the situation as correct, and this reinforced him in his decision to halt the offensive. But Auchinleck, who had been present at Maddalena since 22 November, evaluated the operational result of the battle thus far quite differently, and he managed to have its continuation approved. His efforts, along with the British forces' luck in retaining possession of their supply dumps intact, were probably the decisive factors in the battle's outcome.

On the German side, Rommel certainly believed that he had discovered and hit the Eighth Army's soft spot. This is revealed in his decision to deploy battle groups in the direction of Maddalena and Mersa Matruh. His subsequent abandoning of this part of his plan is attributable largely to the great depth and breadth of the *DAK*'s dispersal; the clear increase in successful enemy aerial activity; and the greater than expected number of enemy troops encountered. These factors no doubt led him initially to keep his forces concentrated in the attacking spearheads. Not immaterial to his considerations was also the fact of his and General Crüwell's being inadvertently stranded overnight behind British lines east of the border wire, surrounded by the enemy and nearly captured, being able to regain German positions only the next day. Further affecting his thinking was the months-long preparations he had made to have his forces positioned around Halfaya, Sidi Omar and Bardia hold out if they were, in turn, isolated and cut off. He'd promised to return and cut them out, even if that were to take weeks. Now that had transpired. He had pushed into the British depth with the *DAK*, indeed he stood in the enemy's rear and was in contact with the fortress troops of *Abschnitt Ost*.

The prevailing operational situation was now characterised by the fact that each side could decisively threaten the other's supply lines. In the wake of initial losses, the desert's open spaces and the great distances from their respective bases of supply to front-line combat units forced the opponents to secure their weaker elements with individual heavy weapons. In light of such vulnerabilities, German forces developed something of a new way of fighting, one based partially on the British example, in which troops not immediately engaged in earlier fighting were now to be drawn in. Such troops served as roving security-and-reconnaissance formations, and consisted of small numbers of tanks or other armoured vehicles, artillery and trucks. Later to become a standing part of moving columns, these troops interfered with each side's resupply efforts. They also sometimes surprised even enemy combat units. In the process, they often left behind them unpleasant results for commanders on both sides, not least with the destruction of vehicles. In turn, however, resupply columns began to incorporate their own armoured vehicles or anti-tank guns for protection. Consequently, the fighting spread ever further afield, and the entire area between the Trigh el Abd and Via Balbia became increasingly dangerous.

At the time, Rommel did not appreciate this development. The German panzer forces were blind in any case, since the *Luftwaffe* had only three aircraft available for reconnaissance on 24 November. Thus, the German panzer troops were provided no clear picture of the operational situation. The commanding general's communications link with his principal operations officer at headquarters at El Adem were also faulty. Rommel therefore determined on his own that his mission for 25 November consisted of completing the enemy's destruction by the *DAK* in the general area of Sidi Omar–Sollum.

At this juncture, Rommel still counted on certain results from the defeats he had inflicted upon the British over the preceding two days. He initially expected the enemy to continue to withdraw to the south-east. He would intercept this movement on a broad front from the area about 10km south of Halfaya Pass and stretching to the Trigh el Abd and about 30km west of Sidi Omar. The 21st Panzer Division was stationed in the east, and the *Ariete* Division to the west. In the centre he would direct an attack intended to accelerate the breaking up of the British offensive that would also retake Sidi Omar. The two reinforced panzer regiments were tasked with the mission, forming up in a separated arrangement to take that place. Meanwhile, the bulk of 21st Panzer Division remained at the ready south-west of Halfaya Pass to intercept the anticipated enemy breakthrough to the east from either Sidi Omar or Capuzzo.

The *DAK*'s attacking elements made early contact not only with the 7th Indian Brigade and its reinforcements around Sidi Omar, but also with the 2nd NZ Division. With their tanks in deep echelon, the New Zealanders had been covering British operations near Capuzzo, Bardia and further to the north-west. Throughout, the German forces stood under repeated aerial bombing and strafing. The 5th Panzer Regiment fought hard but with little ground gained. The 8th Panzer Regiment also encountered British armour which, though destroyed, gave proof of increasing resistance. Recognising this situation at about 0900 hours, Rommel sought to encircle the enemy and destroy him using 15th Panzer Division. This would bring him his expected victory. But he simultaneously realised that the British Eighth Army was not weakened nearly so much as he had thought earlier that morning.

Echeloned deep to the west, 15th Panzer Division bypassed Sidi Omar to the west, but here, too, those echeloned elements were hit by interspersed artillery fire and armoured attacks coming from the east. In this case, 8th Panzer Regiment reported that its tanks and flak guns had destroyed 16 attacking British Mark II tanks. Captured British POWs revealed that they were from the 7th Armoured Brigade. Nevertheless, bombing attacks hit the *DAK* hard, especially when its units stopped to refuel, as they did at about 1230 and 1600 hours. By evening, however, the division's spearheads reached the Trigh Capuzzo to the west of Sidi Aziz, and thus succeeded in encircling the enemy near Sidi Omar and Capuzzo to a depth of some 30km north to south.

Throughout the same day, 5th Panzer Regiment had attempted unsuccessfully to take several British strongpoints near Sidi Omar from the south. Neither changing axes of attack nor encirclement using fire and manoeuvre brought the regiment victory. The battle's intensity is revealed by a radio message sent at about 2000 hours:

> 'Strongpoint Cirener still hard fought. Now 8km south-west of Sidi Omar. 5th Panzer Regiment still has 12 tanks; only 2 operational. Regimental CO killed. Battalion CO missing. Request orders.'

The *DAK*'s encirclement and assault had brought no decisive success. The 8th Panzer Regiment had 53 tanks ready for operations, the 5th Panzer Regiment only two. British aerial attacks increased. The *Ariete* Division was still blocked west of Gabr Saleh by the 1st SA Brigade and other units of the 4th British Brigade. Lengthy supply lines running clear through the enemy's ground only made matters worse. Both German divisions registered shortages rapidly increasing by the hour. At the same time, the divisions were forced to send out search parties to find the supply columns during their long and dangerous approach marches.

The initial arrangement of forces on 25 November also demonstrated that the German commander did not have operational clarity of the situation. He had assigned missions the night before for movement by combat units against the supply dumps at the desert railway's terminus at

Habata and at Maddalena to the south. These plans could not be carried out during the day. He had also ordered 21st Panzer Division (minus 5th Panzer Regiment) to march against Halfaya Pass from the south. Since their supply vehicles had been unable to find them in time, however, these units were not ready to go until 26 November.

Rommel's orders to the *DAK* therefore changed from pursuit of British forces at an operational level to the fighting of a tactical battle of annihilation around Sidi Omar. Two sets of impressions appear to have influenced Rommel's decision-making. On the one hand, there were the effects of his having been forced to hide out behind British lines east of the border wire. There he saw heavy British supply and communications traffic first-hand. Even armoured reserve columns passed by the stranded vehicle in which he, General Crüwell and his chief of staff spent a long night. The enemy appeared to be anything but beaten. In the following days, Rommel made a virtue of necessity by using a captured British command car to travel repeatedly across the lines and being either sufficiently unobtrusive or too lately recognised.

Rommel's insistence on dashing from unit to unit to deliver orders personally derived not only from the urgency which he believed was necessary to force the enemy to his knees, but also from a lack of sufficient oversight of the battle brought on by deficient long-distance communications. Radios failed either because of the too-great distances between them or, more frequently, because their batteries ran down. Used for periods of several days, they had to be changed all too frequently. Replacement batteries, however, were often far to the rear or the vehicles delivering them went missing. In any event, the general did not receive the updated information sent over the air by his command centre, which lay more than 100km to the west in El Adem. From there, the *Panzergruppe*'s operations officer attempted to oversee the situation in the entire battle compartment. Thus, in agreement with Rommel, he too thought on 25 November that the enemy should be pursued and destroyed, as indeed that task had been begun the day before. His radio message of 25 November at 2257 hours – which evidently was not picked up by the receiving station – shows clearly the sorts of problems that arose from too great a physical separation of the tactical commander(s) from the command centre:

25.11.41
2257 hours
From: *Panzergruppe Afrika Ia* (Operations)
To: General Crüwell
Is situation map gone? – Tobruk quiet. – Böttcher repels attack by 2 armoured battalions of reinforced New Zealand divisions at Hill 55. – Enemy south-west of el Gubi. – Evidently 2 brigades, [plus] elements of armoured brigade diverting in part to south-east. – Beginnings of withdrawal by elements midday. – Elements 2nd South African Division moving south-west 25.11. 0700 hours via Sidi Barrani. – *Pavia* [Division] old position, de Meo 57/6. – *Trieste* [Division] with Böttcher 50 minus regiment. – Request situation on Sollum front and commander's intent. – Until now having to send almost all messages blind. – What direction should Böttcher and *Trieste* follow tomorrow if necessary? – Recommend east.

Panzergruppe Ia.

A commander's movement, however, can also create other problems. By hurrying from one critical point to another, he may well be able to affect the outcome at any given moment in a specific location, but he could hardly coordinate all his forces in time and space over the long term. Consequently, it happened that Rommel's activity in issuing orders on the spot to various armoured units did not always mesh well with the directives provided by the commanding general of the *DAK* himself. Even though the same tactical thinking existed at various levels of command, inconsistencies in combat units' dispositions occurred. This condition is illustrated in 21st Panzer Division's being ordered by Rommel on 25 November to take Halfaya Pass but being unable to comply due to supply problems. In a radio message from the commanding general on 26 November, these orders were changed. The division was to bypass Halfaya and Sollum, and advance from the south to Bardia. It is possible that this particular order was misunderstood. Nevertheless, it was executed in this fashion, even though Rommel needed the division further to the west, and the *Panzergruppe*'s operations officer ordered the division back early the next day.

D. The Crisis South-east of Tobruk

On this day, 25 November, *Kampfgruppe Böttcher*, formed earlier from the 104th Artillery Command, had to prove itself in defensive actions around Bel Hamed and to the south of the Via Balbia. The 2nd NZ Division's brigades, supported by tanks, drove hard against these positions but were repeatedly repulsed. The troops of the German 155th Rifle Regiment and the 361st *Afrika* Regiment were ably supported by artillery positioned south-east of Tobruk. A serious situation nevertheless presented itself for the Germans due to a lack of anti-tank guns, particularly in the *Afrika* Regiment. Still, the German defences held steady, due in part to effective support by those *Luftwaffe* aircraft that were operational. These attacked at crucial junctures in the fighting, a participation made possible by the nearness of the *Panzergruppe's* central command post and the clearly delineated front lines. This assistance partially offset the Germans' weakness in those anti-tank guns which either had not yet been shipped from Italy or which lay at the bottom of the Mediterranean. For the units under the command of the Division *zbV Afrika* defending the Via Balbia westward toward Tobruk and eastward, the situation was quiet. A new factor, however, was the naval gunfire support provided by British warships in the roads off Tobruk's harbour, while aerial attacks also inflicted increasing losses in both personnel and matériel. Still, though only with great effort, all British attacks from the east were beaten back.

The general staff officers at the German headquarters at El Adem were evidently well apprised of the battle's development. In fact, the day's reports led them to conclude that the enemy was building his forces steadily south-east of Tobruk and that a growing threat of a breakthrough to the city was present. Of course, the British would certainly view any such link-up as a victory for their offensive. This serious development only came to Rommel's attention early on 26 November due to the faulty communications. At this point, the situation around Tobruk, when combined with increasing disruption of the *DAK*'s supply lines and heavy British air attacks throughout the battle area, must have reinforced Rommel in his decision to try to complete the enemy's destruction as quickly as possible between Sidi Omar and Capuzzo. He appears to have been weighing options that would arise afterwards. On the one hand, he could undertake a general pursuit of enemy forces into Egypt proper. Conversely, he could intervene south-east of Tobruk with the *DAK* if – contrary to his expectations – the German troops fighting there failed to master the local situation.

For their part, in the preceding two days British commanders had managed to bring order to the 7th Armoured Division and 1st SA Division. Now the 6th and 4th NZ Brigades were pushing from the east into the area of Bel Hamed and to the south of that place. The 7th Indian Brigade had successfully defended itself in Sidi Omar, and the 5th NZ Brigade was prepared by means of all-around defense to fix German forces in place near Bardia and, principally, at Capuzzo. The two sides had thus extended their strongpoints, staff objectives and supplies across the entire coastal plain, from the sea to points south of the Trigh el Abd. Both sides were operating in the enemy's territory, and both sides knew it. Roving combat patrols scored kills on both sides, and the RAF exploited its opportunities to the full.

South-east of Tobruk, the defensive battle of *Kampfgruppe Böttcher* and the Italian *Bologna* Division against an enemy of growing strength entered its next, more intense phase. The New Zealanders remained stubbornly in contact, keeping up their attacks even after sundown, and took Bel Hamed during the night of 26 November in a tank-reinforced assault. At 0630 hours, troops in the Tobruk perimeter attacked with the support of 50 Mark II tanks and overran El Duda. In a heavy, swirling battle, a successful counterstroke to the north by Italian Bersaglieri of the *Trieste* Division allowed *Kampfgruppe Böttcher* to hold its positions initially. In the afternoon, however, 30 British tanks were able to make contact with the New Zealanders at Bel Hamed, although at first only for a few hours. Thereafter, German and Italian troops in turn succeeded in once again breaking through the link–up. The fighting was very costly to both sides, and both German and British reports indicate the loss of 26 British tanks. For the Germans, the lack of anti-tank weapons nevertheless made itself felt, and the British continued their attacks after darkness fell. Weakened German and Italian blocking forces could no longer hold. As a result, *Kampfgruppe Böttcher* relinquished control over the corridor, fell back southward to the rear of the *Trieste* Division and there established a rally-point. For their part, the New Zealanders established contact along the axial road with the troops inside the fortress.

Attrition of the DAK at Capuzzo and Bardia

Early on 26 November, the operations officer of *Panzergruppe Afrika* at El Adem attempted to apprise the *DAK* of the renewed seriousness of the situation near Tobruk. Liaison aircraft were shot down, however, and radio contact with 21st Panzer Division was established only with difficulty, and then only for a short time. As a result, that officer took it upon himself urgently to order the return of the division to the area of Tobruk. Nonetheless, the issuing of the order and its eventual receipt can no longer be clarified precisely. Having dispatched the reinforced 15th Panzer Division in the direction of Bardia for the destruction of the New Zealanders, Rommel assumed that 21st Panzer Division was south-east of Halfaya Pass in keeping with his last order. However, this division broke through the Indian troops, bypassed the German forces at Halfaya Pass, moved east of the minefields and attacked the 5th NZ Brigade late in the day with some elements out of Sollum, while other divisional units joined with 15th Panzer Division.

The *DAK* recognised as early as the night of 26 November that positioning the 15th Panzer Division in depth had made no sense; that the enemy's expected collapse hadn't occurred; and that there were no enemy forces capable of fleeing for the Germans to intercept between Sidi Omar and Sidi Aziz. Consequently, with Rommel's approval, the division was pulled together in the north to renew the attack on Capuzzo at daybreak. The serious supply situation, however, prevented this. There remained no other choice than to gain the area around Bardia so as to renew stocks of fuel, ammunition and provisions. By about 1200 hours, the division found itself there. It refitted and seized substantial portions of matériel there, but there was little sign of the enemy himself. Late in the day, the 115th Rifle Regiment was in position to launch the attack on Capuzzo. As twilight fell, the infantry were able to break into and overrun the enemy's field fortifications. Despite several counter-attacks and intense, close-quarters fighting, the leading elements stood 800m from Capuzzo in the face of an enemy giving ground. At that point, Rommel broke off the attack and withdrew the rifle regiment to their jump-off positions of the afternoon. At the same time and to the east, 21st Panzer Division's approach from Sollum became evident. The *Ariete* Division had also, finally, extricated itself from the fighting around Gabr Saleh. It reported its position in the area that evening 35km west of Bardia.

British aircraft had inflicted heavy losses on the Germans, particularly on their supply columns. This affected 21st Panzer Division most severely, and the *DAK*'s units once again experienced concerns over their resupply. Rommel, present as he was with 15th Panzer Division in Bardia, may not have had a complete appreciation of the general situation. His plans had been disrupted by 21st Panzer Division's arrival in Upper Sollum and Bardia. His breaking off the night attack on Capuzzo illustrates how he was surprised by the nighttime situation of his forces. He would further have seen how the intensification of the fighting around Tobruk; the melting of the *DAK*'s strength; that corps' supply situation; and, not least, British air superiority were all forcing him to alter his plans. Still, he did not yet draw the full conclusion from the situation, even though his calculations did not entirely go up in smoke as they had done the previous night. Thus, he ordered 21st Panzer Division to push west along the Via Balbia on 27 November. At the same time, 15th Panzer Division was to complete the destruction of the enemy to the division's front by driving south through the area of Sidi Aziz–Capuzzo–Sidi Omar.

The Situation on the Night of 26 November

The headquarters of *Panzergruppe Afrika* calculated that its own total losses had been high. That said, it also acknowledged the capture of the commander of the 1st SA Division and several thousands of British troops in the fighting. During the same night – 26 November –Auchinleck returned to Cairo. There he replaced Eighth Army's commander, Cunningham, with General Neil Ritchie.

In the British XXX Corps, many elements had used the pause in the fighting since 24 November to collect themselves, regroup and reorganise in the area along both sides of the Trigh el Abd. Auchinleck's evident desire to carry on the fight inspired his men and gave impulse to the armoured formations' efforts to refit and recuperate. Their fighting strength was significantly renewed from deliveries of new tanks, and they had already been invigorated by the successes of their roving combat patrols and effective air cover. Their lethargy of 23 and 24 November therefore gave way to a determined willingness to carry on with the offensive. In this, the success around El Duda also played a role. Though the corridor into Tobruk in this sector was only about 1.5km in width, the British troops had driven both the Division *zbV Afrika* (in the north) and *Kampfgruppe Böttcher* (in the south) completely onto the defensive. Only by the greatest efforts were the German troops able to prevent the corridor being widened.

Even so, XXX Corps now began to direct its attention to its own eastern flank, and the 2nd NZ Division stood guard in the rear. It was here that the *DAK* was to be expected, and the British began adjusting for a defensive battle west of Gambut–Gabr Saleh. While *Kampfgruppe Böttcher* still stood under significant enemy pressure in the early hours of 27 November, the fire later gradually subsided. The German forces thereupon immediately attempted to fix the British in place, in some sectors successfully, but after about 1100 hours, quiet returned along the axial road at El Duda due to general exhaustion.

It was clear to *Panzergruppe Afrika*'s operations staff that the units fighting around Tobruk and Bel Hamed were at full stretch. No reserves were available. The British had succeeded in breaching the ring around Tobruk, and the fighting to the south was making a catastrophic defeat for German forces ever more probable. A radio message of clear import thus went out between 1630 and 1800 hours, one which the *Panzergruppe*'s commander must have received at least in part:

From: *Panzergruppe Afrika Ia*
27.11.41
To: Commander
    0557 hours
Kampfgruppe Böttcher with heavy loss back on both sides. Allow 8th Panzer Regiment come immediately. Recovery [of the situation] possible only thereby.

Panzergruppe Afrika Ia

From: *Panzergruppe Afrika Ia*
27.11.41
To: 21st Pz Div
　　0557 hours
Situation Tobruk great danger. Immediate appearance of even individual elements 21st PzDiv of decisive importance. Report when appearance possible. Remain in standing radio contact.

Panzergruppe Afrika Ia

From: *Panzergruppe Afrika Ia*
27.11.41
To: 15th PzDiv
0600 hours
Cannot contact commander this hour. *Panzergruppe* orders immediate appearance for relief Tobruk front. Situation great danger. Attention.

Panzergruppe Afrika Ia

However the messages may have been received, their tone regarding the situation at Tobruk was unmistakable.

The DAK Thrusts West

From Bardia, 21st Panzer Division appeared along the Via Balbia during the night, having been able in the meantime to scrape together enough fuel and ammunition. All elements of the *DAK* nonetheless suffered from supply shortages. Scant numbers of supply vehicles, made up in part from inventory east of Tobruk and often halting north of the Via Balbia, drove into the area around Bardia. Supplies already in Bardia also had to serve as a source of resupply. After some delays caused by overlapping march routes with 15th Panzer Division, 21st Panzer rapidly gained ground to the west. It reached Gambut against varying degrees of resistance, and only about 8km further to the west did that resistance, by both British and New Zealand troops, noticeably stiffen in the afternoon.

The 15th Panzer Division understood the radio message from the *Panzergruppe*'s operations section as a change of mission and prepared to go forward along the Trigh Capuzzo to the left rear of 21st Panzer Division. Moving south by west from Bardia, it completely surprised and overran the command post of the 5th NZ Brigade near Sidi Aziz. The New Zealanders' commander and 500 troops, as well as six guns, baggage and other supplies, were captured. Joining the division shortly thereafter, Rommel approved the march to the west. He nevertheless insisted that the 115th Rifle Regiment should simulate further groups of forces by striking out southward and moving past Capuzzo and Sollum. Further, he ordered the reinforced 33rd Combat Engineer Battalion to launch an attack to surprise the enemy in Capuzzo itself.

In the first half of this rather dull, cool day, the bulk of the division moved south-west and quickly gained the Trigh Capuzzo in the direction of Tobruk despite numerous British low-level aerial attacks. The division's leading elements repeatedly came into loose contact with the enemy, and artillery fire frequently became unpleasant. The British 4th and 22nd Armoured Brigades frequently attacked and belaboured the division's flanks, but it reached the area around Gasr el Arid in the evening and that night assumed a 'hedgehog' position south of Sciaf-Sciuf. As a result of the enemy's stiffening resistance further north, 21st Panzer Division also sought support in that direction. Meanwhile, the 33rd Combat Engineer Battalion's attack against Capuzzo lasted into the night but remained unsuccessful, and the 115th Rifle Regiment had waited on it. Both units subsequently repaired to Bardia for resupply and received orders during the night of 27–28 November to return to the division. Nevertheless, Rommel, evidently believing on the afternoon of 27 November that he had broken the enemy's back at both Bardia and Sollum, turned his gaze definitively to the west.

Since the armoured *Ariete* Division moved in echelon to the left rear and south of the Trigh Capuzzo, the *DAK* stood on a broad front south–west of Gambut facing an enemy to the west. With the mass of the 2nd NZ Division, the British still held Bel Hamed, Sidi Rezegh and the airfield. For his part, Rommel had pushed his command post forward to a point near Gambut. Now once again in direct radio contact with his main headquarters at El Adem, he learned of the *Panzergruppe*'s operational situation. It appeared to verge on complete collapse due to the attrition caused by the fighting for the corridor which the British had opened into Tobruk; the enemy's air superiority; catastrophic shortages of supplies; and, not least, losses of both personnel and matériel.

E. The Bel Hamed Pocket

The broad-front attack had clarified the tactical situation for the German armoured commanders. Between the *DAK* and the troops besieging Tobruk stood primarily New Zealand units, and the enemy's armoured formations still operating to the south did not appear to have been organised in a unified fashion. Thus, it seemed that a favourable opening had been provided for action in the areas of Sidi Rezegh and Bel Hamed.

On 28 November, under lowering skies and rain, 21st Panzer Division attacked towards Point 175 and Zaafran. The enemy's forces defended themselves resolutely but were encircled from the east. At the same time, the panzer division sought to link up with the Division *zbV Afrika* – now renamed the 90th Light Division – on the northern front. To the left, 15th Panzer Division also attacked. It gained the heights south of Sidi Rezegh (8km south of Bel Hamed) and energetically drove back British tanks which had been thrown in almost individually on the Germans' flanks. In the process, many hundreds of German POWs were freed. In addition, concentric attacks made in conjunction with the *Ariete* Division forced away enemy troops who had driven into the seams between the attackers. Though bad visibility, including fog, made proper recognition of friend and foe difficult, the *DAK* nonetheless registered an essentially accurate picture: enemy armour stood all around. Nonetheless, that night the *DAK* believed it had good prospects for encircling the British and New Zealand troops on the by now familiar battlefield of Sidi Rezegh, but the many local movements and adjustments that had to be made by both sides demonstrated that the British had managed on 28 November, for the first time, to push a relief column into Tobruk.

At this time, the British armoured forces, especially 7th Armoured Division, remained generally on the southern flank of the battle area. The division was thereby in direct connection by way of the Trigh el Abd with its bases of supply to the south and south-east, an important fact.

The division was still refitting in the wake of its heavy losses in personnel and equipment since 20 November. Once again, the British went about the process in systematic fashion. Operational capability depends not only on units' replenishment but also on the precondition of ensuring that the apparatus of command is properly engaged. That part of the process takes longer. At such a time, only those combat actions are possible which serve to familiarise troops and commanders with the enemy and with prevailing combat conditions, but these actions must be possessed of a tenacity that can be turned to good offensive use. Thus, seemingly unconnected operations at the levels of companies and platoons can become active seasoning actions allowing for the troops involved to fight even more effectively later. The situation demanded it. For the moment, the British XXX Corps could only deploy elements up to battalion strength on the *DAK*'s southern flank. These nevertheless could serve to deflect their German counterparts and fix them in place, but British respect for the Germans' armoured formations was evidently greater than one had expected. More energetic British action could have prevented further tactical successes for a *DAK* which had itself been weakened in the preceding 10 days. That said, the British resupply effort remained unmolested. No enforced improvisations were required as replacement personnel and bulk items were brought up from Egypt. The emphasis which the new commander of the British Eighth Army placed on the idea of the offensive began to make itself felt. The leadership of the army's corps became steadier, and the strategic reserve – the 2nd SA Division – was pushed forward to a point south-east of Maddalena. Only the exposed Battlegroup E in the oasis of Gialo was subjected to repeated German aerial attacks. As before, it would assume no importance in the British offensive.

For his part, Rommel returned by plane to El Adem before noon. That would not be without favourable results for the Italian commanders whom he could reach from there. For his orders for 29 November, the question was of no little importance whether the British and New Zealand forces near Sidi Rezegh would be thrown into the fortress [presumably *Tobruk*] or kept separated from it and then isolated and encircled. The *DAK*'s commanding general was evidently inclined to the first outcome, more promising as it seemed to be of success. Rommel nevertheless pursued the more daring response with the mobile German forces.

While 21st Panzer Division remained caught up in stubborn fighting during 29 November on both sides of the Trigh Capuzzo, 15th Panzer Division drove to the south past the New Zealanders in one go, surprising them in the process. The division shattered the 1st SA Brigade's flanking attacks and ended up in the operational area of *Kampfgruppe Böttcher* and the Italian XXI Corps. In the afternoon, the division turned north and, using all the combined arms at its disposal, attacked the enemy along the axial road from the south–west. Even though the British artillery attempted to contest every foot of ground with uninterrupted fire, El Duda was taken. German dismounted infantry became separated from their armour. Again and again, German armoured vehicles helped carry the infantry's advance by providing mobile, armoured covering fire. In its turn, the rifle regiment ended up with barely 150 men to cover the tanks on both sides by El Duda. After darkness fell, the mechanised infantrymen proved too weak to fend off the enemy's attacks, particularly after their own tanks withdrew from the captured high ground to replenish their stocks of ammunition. Consequently, when enemy tanks and infantry attacked at about 2230 hours without heavy preparatory fire giving away their intentions, El Duda was once again lost. The rifle regiment's few anti-tank guns and artillery pieces were lost, and fully half of the infantry were taken captive.

On the southern front, the uncoordinated attacks of the British 7th Armoured Division and the 1st SA Division against 15th Panzer and the *Ariete* Division resulted in heavy fighting, but remained without success. On that same south–eastern flank, 21st Panzer Division was also attacked and compelled to commit more forces there than against the New Zealanders. The most serious British armoured thrust, likely by 4th Armoured Brigade, fell in the afternoon on *Kampfgruppe Böttcher* even as 15th Panzer attacked El Duda to the north. Of 100 enemy tanks, *Panzergruppe Afrika* registered 20 kills. That night, British forces withdrew once more to the south. In the meantime, 90th Light Division attempted to help close the corridor by fire and manoeuvre and by plugging gaps. In the afternoon, the division deployed its then-only-available assault force, an anti-tank company, with which it gained good ground around Bel Hamed. Nonetheless, no link was established that day with 15th Panzer Division.

Once again, the *Panzergruppe* enjoyed a favourable tactical situation. The mass of 2nd NZ Division, along with elements of 7th Armoured Division, was closed in; the corridor into Tobruk was nearly sealed off; and all the British armoured attacks on the southern flank had been driven off with heavy losses. Still, Rommel and his staff did not conceal the fact that the Germans too had suffered greatly. Resupply was bad due to shortages of both fuel and ammunition; supply routes had become ever longer and more dangerous; and units' refitting was too close to the front to be reliably effective. To make matters worse, 21st Panzer Division's commander, General von Ravenstein, had been captured that morning by the New Zealanders while driving through an area supposed to have been cleared of enemy troops. The garrisons of Bardia, Sollum and Halfaya Pass were again encircled, and the *Luftwaffe* could only fly limited missions at critical points due to its few available aircraft. In contrast, British airpower continued to be greatly superior in numbers and capable of inflicting serious damage. Given this realisation, the *Panzergruppe* remained firm in its intention to destroy the encircled 2nd NZ Division. At the same time, measures were begun to evacuate the depots and resupply points lying between Tobruk and Bardia and to reinforce the bases west of the line running from El Adem to Bir el Gubi.

On 30 November, the Germans renewed their concentric attacks against the encircled New Zealanders, who continued to resist bravely. The point of main effort was shifted south-east from El Duda, not only to allow Sidi Rezegh to be taken by *Gruppe Mickl* (formerly *Böttcher*) attacking from the south-east while 15th Panzer Division came on from the south–west, but also to deceive the enemy. The 15th Panzer, however, was not ready early in the day as planned. Following an incorrectly deciphered order, it had begun moving to the west and withdrawing from the battle. It now had to reverse its line of march and was ready to step off only at midday.

In addition, British bombers were once again active as the weather turned clear. Aiding them was the confined area around the steep escarpment near El Duda, Sidi Rezegh and Bel Hamed, as well as the open space between the opposing armies that was caused by stand-off duels between the two sides' tanks and artillery. Numerous heavy bomber attacks struck the German troops attempting the encirclement. Further, the heavy guns of the New Zealanders' positions and those of the garrison in Tobruk and at Sidi Muftan could reach the Germans, just as the Germans' could reach them. The British, however, enjoyed a superiority in numbers. Consequently, the Germans made no gains in the first half of the day, and as 15th Panzer Division appeared on the scene in the afternoon marching northward to turn Sidi Rezegh from west to east, it became bogged down in fierce fighting. Only the intervention of *Gruppe Mickl,* the 8th Machine Gun Battalion and the 8th Panzer Regiment, attacking from three sides simultaneously, broke the New Zealanders' resistance in close-quarters combat. Nevertheless, while the Germans succeeded in blocking the British corridor into Tobruk, they could not eliminate it. El Duda remained in British hands. For their part, however, the Germans took 600 prisoners and 12 guns, and gained ground on all sides of the pocket. The New Zealanders were pushed ever more tightly together, and their resistance slackened. On this day, too, British armour repeatedly attacked from the south in the attempt to break the German encirclement. These attacks enjoyed heavy supporting fire, but as before, the British lacked tight and unified control of their forces. Consequently, the hardest-hit Axis forces – particularly 21st Panzer Division's left wing, the *Ariete* Division and *Gruppe Mickl* — succeeded in thwarting British intentions. These forces beat back all British attacks without having to call upon the reserves consisting of elements of 15th Panzer Division and the *Trieste* Division. The German artillery made a signal contribution to the battle. Its agile fire to all fronts was a visible success, but that success brought no favourable overall decision. Failing to attain the objective of the New Zealanders' relief, British forces outside the pocket searched for other weak spots in the Germans' positions. For example, German reconnaissance reported the enemy's flanking of Bir el Gubi (still in Italian hands) to the west. Further, 21st Panzer Division detected enemy armoured groups increasingly in the rear and on the division's northern flank. The bulk of the British formations, however, were discovered to be south of the Trigh el Abd and south-east of Sidi Muftan behind an armoured screen; they were no longer – or were not yet – sufficiently combat–capable. The night of 20 November – 1 December remained unsettled. The 1st SA Brigade vainly attacked the Germans on Hill 175, and the situation of the hard-pressed NZ Division became untenable. They were ordered to fight their way through to the south-east.

This day also saw *Panzergruppe Afrika*'s commanders become evidently concerned about the battle's outcome. Their forces had been heavily ground down by the continuous fighting. Battalions were now frequently reduced to company-strength, and supplies were short even for these shrunken formations. Shortages of both weapons and fuel were critical. The *Luftwaffe* even failed to provide air liaison officers for tactical air control since 'otherwise the disposition of air force personnel would be lost'.

On 1 December, in thick fog, 15th Panzer Division lay in its assembly area near and to the north of Sidi Rezegh. Ready for action were 8th Panzer Regiment, along with the 200th *Regiment zbV* and 2nd Machine Gun Battalion, all supported by two further artillery battalions from the 33rd Artillery Regiment, a battery of 210mm mortars and the 15th Motorcycle Infantry Battalion. In short order, they were forced to defend themselves to the east against armoured thrusts and enemy fire. In spite of this constant threat on the flank, the German artillery managed to keep the enemy's heads down in the area of Bel Hamed. This sufficed to allow the Germans' tanks and infantry to break into the New Zealanders' positions at about 1040 hours and complete their destruction.

At the same time, *Gruppe Mickl* turned back an attempt north-east of Sidi Rezegh by the British 4th Brigade to push in a relief force. While some of the New Zealanders near Bel Hamed evaded the Germans by moving to the south-east, 21st Panzer Division had to defend itself to the south-east, east and north. The 90th Light Division tried to plug the forward gaps in the front but also found itself fighting a defensive battle on its own eastern flank against enemy tanks. At 1630 hours, tanks of the 15th Panzer Division and the 90th Light Division established visual contact on the axial road. After subsequently eliminating enemy strongpoints lying between them, these units linked up directly. Tobruk was thus once more completely encircled.

The piece of ground around Zaafran then had to be taken so as to break remaining resistance in front of 21st Panzer Division which partially encircled the enemy to the east. Once more, however, a misunderstood order led to 15th Panzer Division's halting halfway after darkness fell. Both the *Panzergruppe* directly and the *DAK* issued orders without coordinating them. This generated consequences, not the least of which was faulty transmission. Nevertheless, enemy resistance gradually ceased. Some of the New Zealanders managed to get through the encirclement, and some were taken prisoner that day or the next.

The pocket in which the 2nd NZ Division found itself was eliminated on the evening of this relatively cool but clear winter's day. Another 1,500 prisoners were taken, as were 26 guns. But all the combatants – Germans, Britons, New Zealanders and Italians – were drained, collapsing in sleep almost next to one another. Their units were worn out, their fuel and ammunition exhausted, their tanks and vehicle destroyed or broken down. A pause settled in over the battlefield.

F. The Battle is Over; The Fight Continues

Thus, *Crusader* ended. The British collected themselves south of the Trigh el Abd and the line Sidi Muftan–Bardia. The 4th Indian Division once again surrounded the German–Italian troops at Bardia, Sollum and in the Halfaya Pass. For their part, the Germans and Italians regrouped their units, brought conquered ground into a kind of order and constructed defensive positions with fronts facing south-east and south. The *DAK*, indeed the entire *Panzergruppe Afrika*, now contained only one formation capable of combat after proper refitting and rest, namely 15th Panzer Division. Its tank strength showed the fact clearly:

> Tanks available, evening of 1.XII: 11 Pz II, 24 Pz III, 3 Pz IV
> "   " 4.XII: 13 Pz II, 28 Pz III, 3 Pz IV
> "   " 5.XII: 12 Pz II, 24 Pz III, 7 Pz IV
> Tanks destroyed in the workshop: 5.XII: 10 Pz II; 15 Pz III, 5 Pz IV

The fighting had come temporarily to a halt, and the Germans would now have to assess their further possibilities. Would their forces suffice for a defence to the south-east of Tobruk and perhaps another attempt at Bardia? Or would a withdrawal from the whole of Cyrenaica become unavoidable? How far could the British go in refitting their forces for combat? Did they still have reserves to throw into battle?

But while this one battle was over, the fighting would go on. Rommel would not readily accept the facts. Since he was concerned about the fate of the Axis forces around Bardia and Sollum, and because he needed to refresh the *DAK*, he initially held onto the area between Bardia and Tobruk. A further incentive was the fact of the enemy's possession of El Duda and his own uncertainty about British actions in the area of Bir el Gubi. Only the coming days' realisation of renewed activity by the British XXX Corps would move him to the decision to reorder his own defences south-west of Tobruk. Consequently, giving up the battlefields of *Crusader* prematurely became necessary by 5 December.

Over the course of a fortnight, both opponents had exhausted their personnel and equipment in a series of fierce manoeuvre battles fought with tanks, artillery, anti-tank guns and aircraft. Into the scales the Germans had thrown their generally superior weaponry and the skill of their panzer leaders. The British had countered with their numerical advantages, reserves which *Panzergruppe Afrika* couldn't match, and a tenacious adherence to their plan of battle. For the *DAK*, the timely availability of fuel and ammunition or, on the other hand, their absence had frequently altered the outcome.

On 3 December, the *DAK* reported 34 tanks as operational, a figure constituting a mere 13 per cent of the total of 18 November. One hundred and sixty-seven tanks and armoured reconnaissance vehicles had been lost completely, and more than 20 per cent were still under repair while, in comparison, the Italians had lost approximately 60 per cent (90 in total) of their tanks. For the British, the Germans recorded that 814 armoured vehicles of all types were out of action for Eighth Army. That amounted to at least 70 per cent, and more likely 85 per cent, of that army's active stocks. About 30 per cent of that figure, however, could be replenished from the British reserves. That said, fewer than 100 tanks and crews were available for operations at the beginning of December. Over and above all these figures, German units also reported losses of:

- 34 anti-tank guns
- 60 mortars
- 41 artillery pieces (40 per cent)
- 8 flak guns (88mm)
- 15 light flak guns
- 334 motor vehicles
- 390 trucks
- 10 heavy prime movers

Comparisons for the British in these categories must be assessed to have been higher. For example, losses of British motor vehicles must have been between 1,500 and 2,000.

As for losses of personnel, German reports do not appear to have been exaggerated. Later reports from December, including the loss of the troops in the Halfaya Pass, came in about the same, and British reports indicated no great numbers of prisoners taken. Thus, the Germans lost perhaps 600 killed, 1,900 wounded and some 2,200 taken prisoner or missing. These figures included 16 commanders. In sum, these losses were below 10 per cent of total personnel available. Then, too, Italian losses to 1 December were not especially high. By contrast, total British losses were between 15,000 and 17,000, including three generals, and more than 9,000 taken captive. Losses of aircraft were registered as

- *Ca.* 127 British (12 per cent)
- *Ca.* 100 German (100 per cent)
- *Ca.* 65 Italian (100 per cent)

The battle resulted in no victory. True, Rommel was forced from Cyrenaica. After refitting and resting, however, German forces succeeded in pushing a weakened Eighth Army all the way to El Alamein in 1942. The desert's war of movement would live on.

The war diary of *Panzergruppe Afrika* should perhaps be given the last word, for it takes a position on both the British Eighth Army's superiority and the *Panzergruppe's* own combat leadership:

At the beginning of the attack, the British Eighth Army enjoyed a superiority over German–Italian forces of approximately 75 per cent in tanks, 750 per cent in armoured reconnaissance vehicles, and 180 per cent in light artillery. Only in numbers of infantry battalions and heavy artillery was this superiority somewhat less, about 30 per cent.

The British air force was stronger than ever. It enjoyed a superiority of approximately 200 per cent in fighter aircraft and approximately 50 per cent for both bombers and reconnaissance aircraft.

The operational leadership of the *Panzerarmee* [*sic*] was guided by the effort to bring its numerically inferior forces to bear at the decisive point and the correct point of main effort and in the most effective possible offensive posture. This effort was somewhat limited by both the nature of a coalition war and the sometimes extremely difficult supply situation. Given the numerical inferiority, it was always remembered that *only an offensive conduct of the battle* could lead to success. As– a result, even in those times when the defensive had to be assumed, it was conducted in a mobile fashion. In the execution of this basic principle, the army's leadership was always determined to defeat and, if possible, to destroy the enemy. Occupying territory and winning ground played no role here. Consequently, it made no difference whether Cyrenaica or Marmarica was temporarily in the enemy's possession. The decisive matter was to maintain the army's strength to counter-attack at the proper moment. Regaining ground temporarily given up was the necessary consequence of a successful counter-attack.

The bravery of both sides was exemplary. It was recognised throughout the world both at the time and decades later. In a similar fashion, their combat was characterised by chivalry. The renown of this battle, however, is bound up in the nimbus of the German commander, General Rommel. In that respect, he stands for all the soldiers who fought there.

V

Conclusion

a) Historical Considerations

1. The well-planned British autumn offensive achieved the intended territorial gains but only by accepting losses that were too great. The German armoured forces, also badly weakened, were compelled to withdraw towards Agedabia. These, however, remained strong enough to reconquer Cyrenaica in the spring of 1942. In this respect, the German–Italian *Panzergruppe Afrika* won the winter campaign.
2. The strategic situation in the North African theatre of operations was decisively affected by *Crusader*. While Axis forces could not be substantially reinforced in 1942, the British used that same period to their advantage. The weakening of German arms that resulted from *Crusader* had consequences for all subsequent campaigning in North Africa. By the time of El Alamein in October 1942, British forces had achieved such a superior strength that the German and Italian armies were driven out of North Africa in March 1943. The American landings in North-west Africa and the German units that were rushed into Tunisia altered neither the relationship of power nor the fate of the Axis in Africa.
3. The result of the *Crusader* battle itself was the postponement of the desired British victory by a year. Initially, German armoured forces repeatedly dominated the battlefield. Nevertheless, the British did realise the goal – operating as they were on the exterior lines of

'Fortress Europe' – of making North Africa the base from which to assault southern Europe.

b) Tactical Considerations

1. Without reconnaissance, every commander of troops in the field is blind. Lack of organic reconnaissance elements must be made good by assigning reconnaissance missions to all other combat units. Without reconnaissance, boldness depends on luck. Reconnaissance, however, promises the bold leader the greater victory.

2. Without airpower, modern battle is impossible. Both defence against aerial attack and support for air forces must be expanded. Operational aerial reconnaissance is imperative. Field reconnaissance – in the form of long-range reconnaissance troops, for example – is expedient.

3. In addition to accounting for space and time, combat missions for large manoeuvre units must afford the possibility of fighting on a *single* battlefield. Herein, decentralised forward movement, units' separation and widely spaced objectives find their limits.

4. Area march best accommodates units moving in open order, as well as dispersed and mixed armoured formations.

5. The armoured commander leads from the front and in the point of main effort. He must remain in standing communication with his staff. Reliance on his staff is an important requirement if he wants to integrate his decisions effectively into operational leadership. Every staff must remain mobile. Staff and troops must not lose contact.

6. No individual unit of a combat arm can fight alone. Units fight together on the battlefield. They are mutually supportive. The weakness of one element is made good by another.

7. Anti–tank and anti-aircraft weapons must accompany both armoured and unarmoured units. Additionally, supply columns without such weapons face decimation.

8. Mobile battles offer a broad spectrum for deception. Creativity belongs here. Regular troops, communications, combat engineers and movement can all generate good results if they are reasonably integrated. Gaps and open flanks nonetheless require attention through reconnaissance, direct observation or security forces.

9. Under no circumstances should a pursuit be broken off due to a supply situation. If a pursuit unexpectedly presents itself, great importance attaches to bringing supply vehicles in train with the pursuing elements.

10. Leaders must understand the limits of man and machine, as well as the availability of supplies. Otherwise, units become overstretched and will find themselves in severe crises and unfavourable battles.

Sources

1. Hill, Russel. *Desert War* (New York: Alfred A. Knopf, 1942)
2. Rommel, Erwin. *Krieg Ohne Hass* (Heidenheimer Zeitung, 1950)
3. Young, Desmond. *Rommel* (Collins, Sons and Co., Ltd., 1950)
4. Connell, John. *Auchinleck: A biography of Field-Marshal Sir Claude Auchinleck* (London: Cassel, 1959)
5. "Deutsche Erfahrungen im Wüstenkrieg im Zweiten Weltkrieg", Studies for the Historical Division 1 and 2
6. Hart, Liddel. *Strategy* (1954)
7. Westphal, Siegfried. *The German Army in the West* (London: Cassel, 1951)
8. "Amtlicher Gefechtsbericht der Panzerarmee Afrika Frühjahr 1942", German Federal Archives, Koblenz
9. "Unternehmen Crusader", Captain George S. Patton, *Armor Magazine*, May/June 1958
10. Von Mellenthin, Friedrich. *Panzer Battles* (London: Cassel, 1952)
11. Von Esebeck, Hanns Gert. *Afrikanische Schicksalsjahre* (Limes Verlag, Wiesbaden, 1950)
12. Moorehead, Alan. *Afrikanische Trilogie*, Volume 2 (Geog Westermann, 1947)
13. Clifford, Alexander G. *The Conquest of North Afrika 1940–1943* (Boston: Little Brown and Comp, 1943)
14. Schmidt, H. W. *Mit Rommel in Afrika* (Munich: Argus–Verlag, 1951)

15. Barnett, Correlli. *The Desert Generals* (London: William Kimber, 1960)

16. Agar-Hamilton, J. A. I. and Turner, L. C. F. *The Sidi Rezeg Battles 1941* (London: Oxford University Press, 1957)

17. Kriegstagebuch No.2, der Kdos der 15. Pz/Div—Führungsabteilung —19/11/1941–15/2/1942

18. Gause, Alfred. "Der Feldzug in Nordafrika im Jahre 1941", *Wehrwissenschaftliche Rundschau*, November 1962

19. Jacobsen, H. A. *1929–1945, der Zweite Weltkrieg in Chronik und Dokumenten* (Darmstadt: Wehr und Wissen, 1961)

20. Jacobsen, H. A. *Entscheidungsschlachten des Zweiten Weltkrieges* (Frankfurt: Bernard and Graefe, 1969)

21. Weichold, E. "Die deutsche Führung und das Mittelmeer unter dem Blickwinkel der Seestrategie", *Wehrwissenschaftliche Rundschau*, March 1962

22. Bauer, E. *Der Panzerkrieg*, Volume 1 (Offene Worte Bodo Zimmermann Bonn, 1965)

23. Senger and Etterlin. *Die deutschen Panzer 1926–1945* (Munich: J. F. Lehmanns, 1965)

24. Senger and Etterlin. *Die deutschen Geschütze 1939–1945* (Munich: J. F. Lehmanns, 1966)

Annotations and Abbreviations

Rgt	Regiment
Btl	Battalion
Arko	Artillery Commander
HQu	Headquarters
DAK	German Africa Corps
Ia	1st General Staff Officer, Chief of Operations
Ib	2nd General Staff Officer, Chief of Supply Group
Ic	3rd General Staff Officer, Chief of Intelligence
RTR	Royal Tank Regiment
Pz	Panzer
Div	Division
Pi	Engineers
Fla	Anti-aircraft guns
Pak	Anti-tank guns
SPW	Armoured Infantry Fighting Vehicle
sMG	Heavy Machine Gun
mot	Motorized (usually wheeled vehicles)
LKW	Truck(s)
Gen	General
M	Major
IR	Infantry Regiment
Abtl.	Detachment / Battalion
Kp.	Company
Kdr	Commander
verst.	Reinforced

21. Panzer–Division

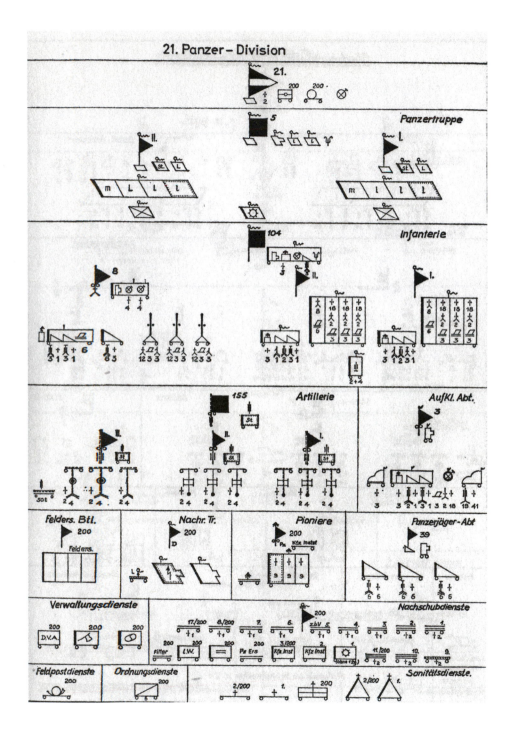

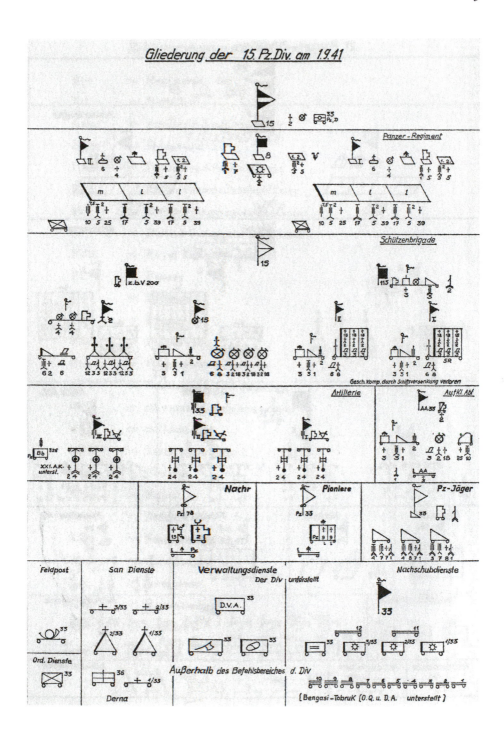

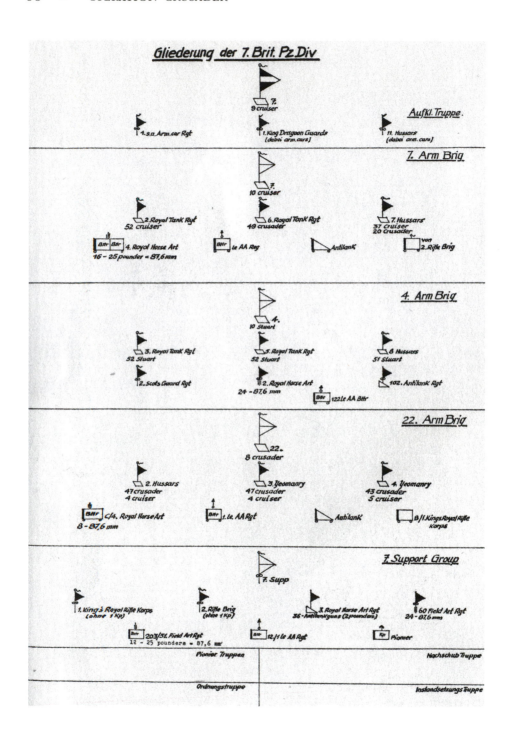

Gliederung der 7. Brit. Pz.Div.

Index